Brittle Branches

By

Randi Gurka

Publication Details

No part of this publication may be reproduced, stored in a
retrieval system or transmitted in any form or by any
means, electronic, mechanical, photocopying, recording,
scanning, or otherwise, except as permitted under Sections
107 or 108 of the 1976 United States Copyright Act,
without either the prior written permission of the author.
Requests to the author for permission should be addressed
online at bbkah@aol.com.

About the Author

After years of struggling in school, Randi was finally able to earn her GED degree. She then went on to graduate Cum Laude from York College with a degree in Psychology and received a dual Master's in Family and Marriage Counseling and School Counseling from Queens College. She became a Guidance Counselor for the New York City public schools and worked for twenty-five years in high school in Queens. After retirement, she went on to follow her passion and became certified as a postpartum doula and a Certified Lactation Educator. This is her first attempt at putting her thoughts onto the written page.

Dedication

This book was written to shed my shell of shame.

To my grand-daughter Zadie Mae:
Home is more than a spot on a map. It is the center where the heart is fixed and from which all feelings and successes radiate.

To my grandson Abraham Rex:
As with every life-altering event we must reevaluate life's priorities. An ounce of weight may not seem to be a lot to many, but if you could have witnessed the joy on your mom and dad's face you would have realized what the real meaning of love and celebration is.

We celebrate each breadth and tear you both have produced. We celebrate your immeasurable bravery, you both are awe-inspiring miracles to your Opa and Oma.

Acknowledgement

Great thanks and appreciation to my husband of twenty-six years, who somehow had the insight to see what I had never seen in myself.

Also great thanks to Ashley and Daniel:
If I only knew what I had always suspected but really did not know, that I had given birth to my own private miracle. Ashley, you have taught me many life lessons. You are strong, determined, resilient, insightful and have so much clarity. With this being said, you somehow were able to search the universe and find Daniel Fellows, the sweetest frosting on the cake. It makes our personal circle of life a wondrous gift. I trust in this gift and would not exchange him for anyone else.

Page Blank Intentionally

Prologue

The psychiatrist proceeded to take out his mildewed smelly textbooks which were the same color as his long finger nails. He quickly turned to his earmarked pages about female genitalia in black and yellow. My dad had said that he would be sitting in the car waiting for me to come out when I was done with the session.

"Does your father touch you here?" I was caught off guard by his question and my brain traveled somewhere safe. I knew he was talking because I saw his mouth moving.

Fat and short with a Hitler like mustache, he tried to tell me why my father did things to me. He kept chattering on, spurting saliva that hit the textbook. My stomach always hurt when I was afraid and just going through those memories frightened me. I hated him and there was no denying why I hated my father so much. I would lie in bed and pray that he would die. I can't even remember the number of times I conjured up different ways for his

1

killing. He had been keeping me home practically throughout elementary school.

My father always told me, "Be a good girl for daddy. I am so afraid to be alone." always starting with "Mommy doesn't take care of me like you do. She is a cold woman."

Being kept home from school had resulted in so many layers of dysfunction. Absent cards arrived weekly but my father would get them before my mother came home from work. Days turned into weeks and I could no longer keep track of the work being taught in class. It was a cycle of me being broken piece by piece and no one had a clue. No friends, crazy family and no one saying anything. I wanted to scream out loud for the world to hear but it seemed my screams had become silenced by my own fear.

I slept in a hi-riser with a metal frame where my legs dangled over, being tall for my age. A hi-riser is built with one bed sliding out from the other and being clicked into the lock position. My sister Lori and I slept in it together. We were so different.

Lori was extremely quiet. A little cherubic, and myopic to the point of being diagnosed legally blind. Her eyeglasses truly looked like the bottom of coke bottles. Lori followed me everywhere. I felt safe when we slept together because I was not accessible to my father. He was careful about that.

I was his comfort, his teddy bear, something he could keep using over and over again. Him lying on me and crying was all too familiar for me. It was a perfectly executed routine so that I could not budge from his weight or the fear that I felt. I was left in a state of confusion when he finished his business. I didn't like it but didn't understand it either, putting me in a weird state of mind. After he was done, special rides to the five and ten were not far away. All the butterfingers were mine. I loved peanut butter and was too young to sense bribery.

Sanford Avenue 1960

One of our neighbors, who had become my friend, lived two floors down from us. "Why doesn't your mom ever cook? All our mothers make Sunday gravy." I really hadn't noticed. I did find myself visiting their place at the same time every Sunday to eat though. Their apartment was a lot different from ours, I realized. There were never smells of baked bread or bubbling sauce that permeated from our apartment, while there was usually something cooking in my friend's apartment. We had to be careful not to get too close to the vat of red liquid boiling on the stove, as warned by my friend's mother. I waited the whole week for that delicious gravy at my friend's place and would start eating it as soon as it was served to us at lunch. It was worth getting scalded on the roof of your mouth with the sesame seeded bread bought that morning.

I was beginning to notice many mundane activities of everyday life, what time families ate, whether there was screaming or silence, how they got along with each other, how long we stood on the landings Monday mornings for the elevator to reach to the sixth floor. This was because I was never good at waiting; I am impatient, edgy and already displaying agitation to those around me. My dad never got ready to go anywhere so it would only be me and my mum waiting for the elevator to go somewhere.

Red brick buildings lined the street where we lived, with perfectly groomed green trees. Everything was linear and appeared in order in our neighborhood. There was a man that lived in this tiny basement room, whose job was to make our hall smell of Lysol. Tenants arrived from the Lower East Side and Brooklyn with dreams of a place similar to our community. Having a man who cleans the landings of each floor was foreign to this new culture of lower middle class, which was something only the good apartments could afford to have.

There were still a few drawbacks such as the excessive noise that came from other apartments around us. The humming of Lionel trains on Christmas morning was as loud as my angry thoughts. *"Don't these neighbors know we are not living in a scene from Miracle on Thirty-Fourth Street?"* I barely existed in these cramped quarters with one sister, no one knew what was happening to me. Spaced so tightly, I continually prayed for the death of one family member, or all of them. It was so suffocating when all four members of our family were in one room. Most often I prayed for the demise of all of us. Despite living in a desirable area, some conditions were deplorable. There was only one bathroom for three females and one ill-kempt man we called Daddy. Walls with tiny pink ceramic tiles begged to be scrubbed. Toothpaste and saliva was cemented to the sink.

Maybe one of the many reasons my mother had no regard for food, cleanliness, rules or schedules was because the emotional holes in her mind and heart were so large they could never be filled. Her constant state of anxiety was palatable. Her mother was the same, and her mother before her. No genetic material for mothering. They did not care about their children or what was happening in their lives, with ice chips running through their veins. They did however care about the male species, wanting their appreciation. They were like a gas tank running on empty, incapable of actual loving when it concerned the children. The irony for both my mother and my grandmother was that they attached themselves to the same type of men. All the men carried the qualities of an empty vessel in a newly sparkled ship. Their capabilities in providing for the family were sparse, leaving their offspring like road kill on the highway.

Our schedules were dictated by my mom's hospital duties. Her garb would always be the same, faded pink housecoat held together with slightly rusted silver snaps. The ride down the elevator tormented my mother as much as the car rides to the hospital. The grinding of the elevator could be heard in the dead of night, along with the desperate cries of my father. I was the one left in charge at such times. Leaving me in charge when I couldn't even take care of myself. "Crying is not going to help. You must take care of your baby sister. I hate him!" she would say to me when I would start crying on her leaving.

My mother and father were heading for another three-day respite. My mother had to face a grueling site whenever she went to the hospital. Psychiatric wards were filled with disheveled men banging on the bars that protected them from escaping. They bawled themselves to sleep until they experienced the calmness as the liquid dripped into their arms. Most of the patients lacked hair making those electrodes easily accessible to their brains. I guess this is why she had gotten used to irregular behavior and found her husband's behavior normal.

Three and half years into their marriage, my mom became pregnant with my sister Lori! The new impending life had given my mom another chance to get it right, a reason to be hopeful. This expanded belly prevented mom from focusing on her despair and heartbreak and helped her look forward. The life she was living was filled with deceit and falsehoods and there was so much she had not been told about my father

My father was born during the depression in the 1930's and was 12 years my mom's senior. He was a tall man with short stubby fingers that were tinted brown from his Lucky Strikes. His hands were smooth and soft from the lack of any sort of work. His persona was one of a baby fawn blinded in the headlights. Women were attracted to him often, but it was vulnerable young girls that made him feel virile. He managed to procreate one more time during their marriage. His stature was tall, lean and strong, but could not bear the weight of his newfound wife and children.

He spoke very little, except when he was having one of his episodes over the choice of what part of the chicken my mother was preparing for that night's dinner or if he would get barricaded after hearing we were expected to get snow.

My father hated chicken; it reminded him of the years his father made him pluck the feathers in their butcher shop that eventually closed due to lack of business. Dad would storm from the table screaming that they were filthy animals and he wasn't going to eat them, whenever my mom made chicken. We would eat in silence after that which is how our meal times usually went by.

Kindergarten 1961

Separation from my mother was actually crushing me emotionally. I would have rather my arm be pulled from its sockets then to be separated from her. I was just in kindergarten and had never been away from her for a long period. Gurgling bile that rumbled in my stomach reached my throat each and every morning anticipating the day's events.

My head would dangle over that Pepto-Bismol color toilet as I wretched, just thinking about the day. Agonizing thoughts overtook my brain, leaving me with disabling anxiety. My appearance was gangly and my complexion had a yellowish hue to it, due to losing body fluids. I became hypersensitive to all sorts of stimuli. Noises seemed louder for me than others. I could hear the barely audible click of the key coming from the door. Footsteps would be recognizable for every member of the household.

If the situation had been different, I would have been amused at my almost super-human acquired powers.

Whenever my father summoned my mom to visit him in the VA hospital, I would become frozen. I truly believed she was not coming back for me. Out of survival in the eyes of society, she needed to function like a caring wife. *"How could she live with herself?"*

My kindergarten was two blocks away from our apartment building. My anxiety was now woven into every fiber of who I am and it seemed I would live with it forever. This is when I became aware of just how unsafe the world was inside and outside. My mother and I were standing in front of P.S. 20 on Sanford Avenue with our new young teacher who was filled with excitement to mold our little minds. My mother accompanied me to our new classroom while I was plagued with terror. Standing three feet away was a brown boy with something shiny and silver hanging from under his long sleeve. *"Captain Hook was in kindergarten!"* I thought to myself. Welcome to my first day of school. I started to cry and gripped my mother's leg. *"Please don't make me go in. I promise I will be a good girl."* I needed to go to school or the police would come and get me. That was what I had been told before coming to school.

My mother was blind to most things in her life. She needed not to see in order to breathe. I am not aware if I actually entered school that day, but eventually I did go. I made a friend in kindergarten, another very quiet girl named Naomi. We sat with each other at lunch. I am not exactly sure what it was that made me feel safe with her. Maybe it was her voice that was soft and didn't hurt my ears. Her dad picked her up from school each day.

He invited me over for a play date one day. I was so happy to have a friend because no one in my family had friends. People were not allowed in our house as there was too much to hide. My father would just sit at our kitchen table in our small vacant apartment doing nothing but smoking his Lucky Strikes back to back all day. He never left the apartment so I guess it was better no one came over. The rooms carried clouds of smoke and the smell of unwashed hair. The sound of my father's hacking coughs would become more and more frequent with the amount of anxiety he was feeling. The only outings he had were the ones to the psychiatrist and the hospital. That's it!

On a random rainy day, Naomi's father asked my mother if I could come over after school. Her reply was *"Maybe another time"* as she didn't know how my father would react to this. That evening, my mother asked my father if I could have this play date.

Our apartment was a two-bedroom apartment with one bathroom. The apartment was barely enough to house five of us. Did I mention that there would be one more daughter conceived nine years later? But we will come to this later. As far as going to Naomi's house for a play date was concerned, how was I to know that this would be an issue? Naomi was the color of sweet caramel candies we got from the counter in the supermarket.

Her voice was quiet and small, she could be friends with anyone but she chose me! No one ever told me that making a friend with a brown girl was a crime no one would ever forget. I was forbidden to remain in contact with her by my father. This incident further polluted the already toxic emotional environment that choked me daily. My manifestations were now becoming physical with migraines, stomach aches and daily vomiting.

We lived seven blocks from the city project named **"The Bland**." All school-aged kids in those projects were zoned for P.S. 20, making our classrooms 50% integrated with children of color, producing a diverse environment.

In second grade, zoning laws changed and I was sent to school miles away from home. Why was I going to school on a bus when my school was two blocks away? No one explained this to me. My mom, disempowered and always silenced, never thought to ask why either. The last thing I needed was another change. This school was totally waspy. You may ask why this was such a bad move for this little Jewish girl? Have I mentioned that I have very curly hair? My hair was yet another reason for my father's disdain of me.

He would direct my mother to fix my hair whenever he looked at me! Apparently, my hair was evidence that I was not his, since my other two sisters had relatively straight hair. He hated everything about me. That was so clear to me from quite a young age.

It was about the eighth year of my life when I started suffering panic attacks. Of course, I had no idea what they were at that time. The feelings they brought on were not much different than how I ordinarily felt. I believe that the physical abuse at my new school was so pervasive that it triggered the panic attacks. The kids at school used me for target practice with their verbal abuse without any recognition from any authority. I was invisible except when someone wanted to take out their rage on someone or something. I would be forced to run as fast as I could just like in the game of tag!

Lining up in size was normal for being counted after lunch. Since, I was the second to last in line followed by Anthony, I was a convenient target. His smell was familiar to me as it reminded me of the way my father smelled after days of not washing. Anthony was so large and mean. His batting practice was hitting me in my back with hard red apples. It hurt so badly, but I wouldn't allow myself to cry. That would make things much worse. Slurs poured out of his mouth; Jew bitch, nigger hair, Olive Oyl. The stigma of receiving free lunch became another burden so I stopped eating.

I was attending a school that was genetically modified consisting of blond straight-haired pretty girls. Heterogeneous grouping had not happened as of yet. I did not want to be in school and I did not want to be home. I felt that I did not belong anywhere. The school projects were where I would usually fit in because people there were conditioned to feeling marginalized and insignificant and invisible. Heroin was on the rise at that time. People risked their lives to get that drug so that they wouldn't feel what I had been feeling forever. I felt alone and hated myself for being born the wrong way in the wrong body. My father's hatred towards me was so contagious that everyone in my family refused to look in my direction.

Dr. Carlesi 1965

My father decided to take me to visit his psychiatrist. As soon as I entered the office, I was aware of a musty smell which seemed to have become a part of the office. The office was dark with old cracked leather furnishings and smelled of cigar smoke and yellow tinted medical books. You know that smell that lingers forever in your brain, it was that kind of an awful smell.

The doctor said a curt *"Hello"* and directed me to have a seat. I, on the contrary, wanted to bolt out of there! I glanced at his fat belly that hung over his belt, my eyes following down to his shiny shoes. He made futile attempts at making me feel comfortable. He held out his left hand while holding down my right hand so hard that I could feel the blood stop flowing. I had a habit of sucking my thumb all the time when I was scared.

As I sucked my thumb, I would press my middle finger cuticle into my upper lip to create a cut. I did this to feel pain and distract myself from the actual pain that people inflicted on me. The doctor observed me in silence while I was doing this.

The psychiatrist proceeded to take out this aged textbook and turned to the page on female genitalia. He asked my nine-year old self if this looks familiar. I did not want to see it but he practically shoved it in my face. *"Does your father touch you here"*? Dr. Carlesi was speaking; I knew he was because his mouth was moving, even though I did not hear him. I think he was saying that my grandmother's hatred for her son, my father, had something to do with me. *"I DON'T UNDERSTAND. I WANT TO LEAVE!!"* I screamed at him, which took him by surprise but he regained his composure immediately.

At this point he asked me to point to the areas on the pictures that I thought my father had touched me. My stomach was hurting and I just wanted to run out of this man's office, who was making me more and more uncomfortable every moment. I then realized that the real motive in bringing me there was to find out if I had told anyone about what my father was doing to me, and I had been thinking that all this was being done to soothe my panic attacks. This VA Hospital doctor was in collusion with my father.

His only concern was to collect payments of two visits per week for the remaining years of my father's life and in exchange he would not disclose that my father was actually a pedophile.

I now could no longer deny or ignore why I hated this man so much. I would lie in bed every night and pray that he would die. I would think of different ways of killing him. He had been keeping me home practically throughout elementary school. My father would instill guilt and shame in me for my mother's behavior of not being a good and attentive wife, and I was too young to understand that none of that was my fault. He would tell me over and over again that he needed me to take care of him since my mother stopped doing so. I continue to smell this man to this day and feel disgusted by it!

I cannot be blamed for having nothing but hate for him, he was the one who made me what I am right now. I was broken from the inside and it showed outside. The two most powerful emotions I felt were pain and anger, which is not normal for a girl of such a young age, to such an extent that I wanted to kill him with my bare hands. Fathers are supposed to protect their children from harm but he was the one harming me, making me face his ugly side again and again.

I went through the constant humiliation and thought I would eventually become numb to it, but I didn't. The only little ray of light in my bleak life was my education but he had even taken that away from me.

The effects of being kept home had resulted in so many layers of dysfunction within me. Whenever I did get a chance to attend school, I was behind in all subject areas. All the students in my class were ahead of me, they knew all the answers while I would sit there looking and feeling dumb. I felt nobody cared about me in school either, except for when they wanted to bully someone. No one knew how I was suffering, going through more and more pain every day. Absent cards arrived weekly but my father would get them before my mom would see them. It was a cycle of me being broken piece by piece. No friends, crazy family and no one saying anything. The silence was suffocating and I had nowhere to go to save myself.

Going home is a feeling of returning to a safe haven for everyone else, but for me it was the opposite. I would feel the pangs of fear and rage grabbing me when I returned home from school and thought of my father. I was his comfort, his teddy bear and he didn't want to lose that by being careless enough to let anyone else find out.

Him lying on top of me and crying was all too familiar. It was perfectly executed so that I could not budge from his weight or the fear that I felt. I was so confused by his sadness and his message of how special I was that I would not move until he was finished. I did not understand his cunning evilness at that time and even if I had, I wouldn't have been able to do anything alone. He was a sociopathic and sympathetic con man.

I found myself being clean and orderly to a fault, maybe to bring some element of normality to my messed up life. I changed my sheets over and over again. I continued to rearrange our bedroom. It gave me a sense of unexplainable euphoria. Changing the sheets remains to be so pleasurable, it seems to be the only thing I can change. Lori on the other hand would come in and destroy all my efforts of feeling clean. She urinated in the bed night after night. Getting her to take a shower was an ordeal.

Substitute

Each attempt at socializing for me was an invitation to the onslaught of panic for my tender emotions. Even when it was deemed a designated safe zone, I would still be frightened by all the people who would be there. My father's anxiety overtook his entire life, making him vulnerable to skepticism because of he could not enjoy the simplest of pleasures. To this day I think he never experienced a true moment of joy in his life due to his condition. It was something on which one would pity him but I think he deserved it, having snatched my innocence and happiness from me.

On the other hand, my mother was a strong woman who firmly stood her ground; she would not allow him to steal her small crumbs of freedom because she was free to do her own bidding with no one controlling her actions. Karen was not going to miss taking off her faded pink housecoat or miss the opportunity to eat someone else's roasted chicken parts. She would never miss the opportunity to dance with a man, even if that man was related to her. She enjoyed these pleasures of life, unlike my father. When finding a man to dance with was not possible, I was her designated partner. As a ten year-old, I would escort her to functions and help her save face. I was her ultimate substitute. If I was not there as her buffer, many people would take the liberty to humiliate Karen for not having a man by her side. *"Where is Al?"* they would ask to mock and make fun of her. Of course, the family secret was not a secret at all. Everyone knew exactly where and how Al was.

One of our favorite times was when someone in the extended family died. Actually when anyone whom we had known died. The reason behind this was a ritual in the Jewish religion called *"sitting shiva."* That is when the immediate family of the deceased would sit for seven days, not including the Sabbath. Mirrors were covered so that vanity is not experienced during the time of mourning. Or maybe you should just not see how fat you are at this time. Not sure, but whatever the reason was, we were not to see ourselves in a mirror. Neighbors, family and friends would come to console the family in mourning. Lori and I called it

"Thanksgiving!" due to the abundance of food we would receive as a way of consolation.

Lori and I were young, around ten and eight years of age. We did not really care about the deceased person, many times not even being sure how we were related to that person exactly. All we cared about was the food. The Kosher chickens, the noodle puddings, the platters of fresh fruit, the chocolate covered almonds and all this delicious food which appeared for us to feast on. We would gorge ourselves on plates of food while waiting for dessert. We anticipated the sounds of dishes being cleared from the table. Timing was imperative to who was going to get those rainbow cookies and chocolate covered almonds.

I couldn't figure out what it was that made the almonds so tempting, so much so that I waited the most for them. Maybe, it was the glistening of the slightly melted chocolate that made them so desirable, rich almond paste and the residue of chocolate on my fingertips. I licked ever so slowly to prolong the flavor on my tongue. All of us in the car ride home reviewed the food. Sadly, we will not have these foods again until the next person dies.

December 12, 1965

This date, the 12th of December 1965, will forever be etched in my brain. It was the day my youngest sister was born. Lori and I came home from school at three o'clock, as usual. We rang the doorbell and waited till our mother came to the door in her pink housecoat. The snaps were not closed. Lori almost knocked my mother down in her attempt to see the new baby in the house. I had no desire to see her or have another human being related to me, so I silently went to my room. Poor baby had no idea what she would experience in her life. I thought I wouldn't care at all about the new addition to our family, however, that changed very quickly.

When Ilyse was a few years old, Mom would return to work and leave me being the responsible elder sister, taking care of everyone and everything like an adult.. Without much of a fight, I was now caretaker of the cutest little girl with the biggest blue eyes, and loved every moment of looking after her. I took her everywhere, to museums, to parks and places I do not recall. I do recall how much I loved her, but never stopped resenting my mother for doing this to us and to herself. At this point in our lives, my parents' marriage was showing signs of obvious neglect. Mom started an affair with an optometrist whom she was employed with. Ilyse was clearly neglected by everyone. The older my mom, Karen, became, the more she resembled Grandma Yetta...looking out only for herself.

Victim 1968

By the time it was 1968, I had truly learned how to be a victim instead of trying to defend myself. I purposely placed myself in dangerous situations probably hoping to get killed or hurt so badly I wouldn't have to live there with my family anymore. That year my mother had a hysterectomy and in those days your stay in the hospital was approximately ten days. Oh no!!!! I can't be here alone with this crazy man that smells of old oily hair that has not been washed in days. This was the primal fear that engulfed me. Did he ever take a shower? I wondered to myself. Or was this his way of knowing just how dirty he was. His penis would often peak out of the slit of his boxers. I fantasized about cutting off his penis and giving him the excruciating pain that he would never forget in his life.

I begged my mother not to go to the hospital. I promised she could trust me to take care of her after the surgery. I was desperate to make her stay any way I possibly could. There was no reason in my twelve- year old eyes that she needed to be at the hospital that long. I cried and pleaded but it did not work. My mother called my grandmother to come stay with us till she was released from the hospital, thinking that she was doing a favor for us this way.

Grandma Yetta

Grandma came to care for us! Instead of her taking care of us, my father took this opportunity to poison her with untruths about me. He told her that I was poisoning my younger sisters. His strategy was to divide and conquer. I felt more isolated than usual. My grandmother would scream at me for every little thing because she believed him. How could my mother's mother believe this man? He was not even her son. But, she believed every little lie he filled her head with. The hurt and anger were enough to drive anyone to despair.

Every Saturday morning, I watched Soul Train, a music show for black teens. Looking at those teens, I would feel inspired because that's how I saw myself. It became a ritual for me. He would not allow me to sit and eat with the family because of my curly afro which screamed at him "Look. Look at your black daughter." Lori and I would sit and watch Soul Train with the volume so low we could hardly hear it ourselves. He came in our room and threw the television onto the floor one day when we were doing this. "Niggers! That's all your sister wants to look at. She is just like them and is going to make you like them too." He continued in his rage.

The next morning, I took the Q44 to Booth Memorial Hospital, laid next to my mother and was hysterically crying. "Please come home", I said. "They are killing me." Of course, that was not a possibility and I knew it but I wanted to try every way I could. "Ok, can I stay here with you? Please." I was very tearful when I asked this, thinking that my mother would understand my situation and help me. "No, they will not let you." She replied solemnly. I was devastated but knew I had to go back to that wretched place we called home.

Homecoming

I was overjoyed and relieved to see Mommy home from the hospital, even though she looked weak and could not walk straight. That did not matter to my father, who did not have an ounce of sensitivity in him. Someone had to go to Social Services and renew our food stamps and that someone had to be mom because my father was too lazy to move. My father's gambling habit now was getting out of hand. One day I came home to a fish wrapped up in a newspaper and thought we were going to have fish for dinner, as naïve as I was. I later found out it was the mob informing him he will be swimming with the fish if he does not pay his debts. I had only heard about the mob or mafia in movies or television shows and didn't believe they could actually be real, until that day.

A few months later, I entered the apartment after school and got the shock of my life. What the FUCK!!! This was a new level of craziness. My father had taken a large can of Nescafe coffee, mayonnaise, mustard and ketchup and spread it all over our greased stained walls and cabinets. I don't know whether he imagined himself to be the next Picasso or had discovered new ways to make our life miserable. I ran into the bathroom and sat on the floor, back against the door so he couldn't get in. I was terrified again, thinking what he could possibly do in this new state of craziness of his. He didn't try the door because he had already done his damage, and left. I came out of the bathroom after not hearing him for a while and when I was sure that he had left. I saw his mental illness splattered as clearly as ever all around me. He was gone!! I came out in disbelief and called my mother at work, screaming at her. "What am I supposed to do with this disaster....?" I knew this was not her fault but it wasn't mine either and I was the one facing it here. I sat down with my head in my hands and no idea how to get rid of this mess.

Visiting Mom's Getaway

I found out that Mom had a lover for a while. It was the optometrist she worked for. My father blamed his tirade on my mother's lack of concern of being discovered. Both of them were starting to resemble each other, if not in looks but in character. Next day, after I came home from school he screamed at me to get into the car. I did so without saying anything because he looked enraged and out of control. I starting crying but that didn't stop him from focusing on his destination. He was driving like a mad man but he knew where he was going.

We didn't go far, a mile or two. I really couldn't see or hear him at this point because of my constant tears, which were not taking a break. We arrived at an apartment building - a red brick typical looking building in Flushing, Queens. My father told me to get out, get out and take a look at where your mother screws her lover! This is where she goes for lunch. I was crying so hard that my tears were burning my eyes. I couldn't believe my ears. Why do I need to know this? I was just a child and their child at that. I was feeling so nauseous I wanted to throw up.

I don't know how he did it but he always found ways to turn my loyalties towards him. This way he could use me as his crying and masturbation platform. I felt so angry that I could kill him yet helpless because I knew I couldn't do anything. How I hated him, yet I felt sorry for him all the time. How could I not comfort him? I had to admit it was quite a powerful position.

The only daughter whom he supposedly hated...yet he yearned for my closeness. This is how he fooled everyone and why no one would believe me even if I ever managed to say something.

I was so confused that I started hating my mother for not doing what she was obligated to do, not only for her husband but for her daughters as well. She distanced herself more and more from her family, as if she had no responsibility towards us. I was pretty sure she felt empowered sleeping with an eye doctor. Big step up from the crazy man she married. She had gotten away from him but what about me.

By this time, I was in fourth grade. I am sure my teachers had a sense that something was not right with Randi. Remember I did not arrive at P.S. 107 until third grade. Constant stomachaches, headaches, and lack of focus were common occurrences. This was not normal for a young child, but there was no apparent reason behind all this either.

On the Jewish holidays, I felt really sad. I never understood why I felt like this. We never practiced any religion or celebrated holidays nor felt part of anything. I would walk by the temple and watch families all dressed up and strolling into the house of worship. Is this what families look like? I had never experienced what it felt like to be part of a normal family. My identity was forming but not through realistic eyes.

I was so confused about myself that I now identified myself as biracial. I was sent away from the dinner table because of the texture of my hair. This was made clear to me from as far back as I could recall. In P.S. 107, the really "white school," they humiliated me daily. Any day I wasn't insulted or made fun of, was not a normal day. Every day we went into the yard for lunch. The kids would separate into the cliques that welcomed them. One day a bunch of kids were playing spin the bottle. I must have felt like I needed to torture myself a little extra that day. I don't know what came over me but I sat down and spun the bottle and Steven said "I am not kissing that ugly thing." Yup, another day of not feeling so good about being Randi.

My sixth-grade teacher, Ms. Berliner, was a tall woman with sensitive eyes. It surely beat the previous year when I had a male teacher. He really put me in a tizzy. It seemed to me that every white man was my enemy. What did they all want? Why did they have a problem with me? What did I ever do to them? Panic set in that year big time.

My attendance was scattered more that year. In sixth grade, I must have barely gotten through because of the frequent absences, but Ms. Berliner promoted me to junior high school anyway. Maybe that was to keep the school from looking like they were not succeeding. Whatever the reason, it was one small thing in my favor. Graduation was upon us and I could no longer keep my rage at bay. I started letting my hair grow out. My mother always kept it short because she had no idea what to do with it.

When extremely curly hair grows, it doesn't grow down it grows out. I starting using a pic (a comb used by African Americans to comb out their hair). It was starting to look like a beautiful afro. BIG, BROWN AND ROUND. This allowed me to look more and more like the people I related to. I felt proud to flaunt something that had been the bane of my existence for so long.

I was angry and I naively thought I would not be harassed at JHS 189. I was terrified of junior high school because I did not know what to expect or what new tortures would await me in that place. I had no friends to transfer with me to my new school. Obviously, I had no friends to speak of so it was an easy transition to transform myself into the new me. A real advantage was I could walk to school. In fact, it was right next door to where we lived.... Sanford Avenue and 147th street.

Rain

One of the few things that I really loved and looked forward to was the rain!!! I loved running out of the apartment leaving my mother and father astonished at my behavior, whenever I would see the sky pouring down. I had started acting out at this stage! For me, this began by going out at night in the blackness of night running through the hardness of the raindrops. The harder it rained, the more I felt cleansed by the universe.

It was not just the smell of the rain that I loved, but I loved the fact that I was getting purer by the water dripping down on me from the heavens. I would randomly run for blocks dripping of beautiful water that fell out of the bushes of curls that surrounded my head. When I returned to the apartment, my father would turn to my mother and always say "Look at your crazy daughter." My mother looked so forlorn and tired wondering to herself what was wrong with her eldest daughter.

I felt that deep down she had to know what a tortured and broken girl I was. My pain was painted so visibly to the naked eye that it should have been impossible for one to miss it, especially someone living with me. My mom related a story to me of when I was two years old. She took me to the prohibitively costly pony rides at Kissena Park. My mother was hoping to see a glimpse of a smile on my face.

Life is supposed to be filled with anticipation, giggles and fun for a child, especially for one so young. However, there was no fun, no smiles ever for me. Looking back, I don't think I knew how to smile even back then. My smiles had vanished so early on that I couldn't even force myself to smile any more. Everyday some sort of new craziness occurred. How do I deal with this? I would continually ask myself this question.

JHS 189

The first day of seventh grade was here and awfully overwhelming. There were so many students from all over Flushing. I was excited as well as terrified because of my previous experiences at school. The neighborhood was changing as slowly as people age. It's a gradual thing that happens, you only notice it when it affects you. Meeting people from Latin America was a new experience, it was different yet interesting seeing the various cultures around us. They really stayed to themselves, which was understandable. I knew how it felt to be different from others and feel others judging you. Imagine how scary it is coming to Flushing from so far away, not knowing anybody, not recognizing the culture of a melting pot or not yet mastering the language.

There we are in the school gym getting our programs and everyone trying to sneak a peek at the other's paper to see if someone was in your class and finding out the scoop on your teachers. That's the common denominator in all schools no matter what language. I

41

looked around at all the different faces trying to determine which of these would turn out to be the bullies, even though I was determined not to get bullied anymore.

Days started to blend into one another like melted chocolate where you look back one day and can't believe so much time has passed so fast. These days affected everyone differently. Some of us curdled, some of us further separated from the general population and then you have the kids that are filled with enthusiasm. Their transition was one of smoothness. Wonder how that feels? I couldn't even begin to imagine how things go so smoothly for some people that they don't even notice the changes.

I however was being bullied yet again, it happens all the time. It is as innate as animals in the wild. They are born to make others feel smaller than they feel themselves. I expected it anyway and it would have been strange if it hadn't happened. The stairway to and from classes was terrible. Who is going to shove so and so down the stairs? It was quite an achievement, especially for me, if I managed to get downstairs without any incident. JHS 189 was not like it was a few years prior, as I had heard. No more SING or recruiting students for the school play. Maybe it did exist but not in my world and I didn't expect to see any improvement either.

Lunch was the place you tried your hardest to put on your armor so that no one can smell the fear. But all those pheromones can be detected by the most skilled predators. I knew I had no chance of being spared if I didn't act fast so I started to gravitate towards some of the tough girls. This way I would be affiliated with strength, not weakness. I didn't want to be the lone one which could easily becomes anyone's prey. The group of girls I joined were a mixed bunch, on almost every level. There were white, Hispanic, black, fat, skinny and even some smart girls in the group and this diversity made me feel even more comfortable.

Most of what other students learned along the way was to not fuck with us! We are "THE SISTERS." Eight to ten females ranging in skills like fist fighting or verbal intimidation. The word spread quickly and no one tried to mess with us. Our "leaders" had decided in one of our meetings that we needed to buy red Eisenhower jackets. They were like military style jackets, which completed the look of a cool girl gang and anybody would think twice before getting on our wrong side. We all had written "THE SISTERS" on the backs of the jackets and the gang became official.

It was not long before the girls found out what a non-violent person I was. Somehow, they did not care and I was grateful for that. All I wanted was protection and I got that just by being a part of the gang. Actually, the smallest one of us was so violent. Once she began to fight she did not stop until she literally saw blood. It sounds a lot more terrifying than it actually was because the ones who messed with any of us usually deserved what they got.

I really felt so brave with these girls backing me, no more worries of harassment. People were actually afraid of us and I couldn't believe they were indirectly afraid of me too as I was a part of the gang. It was an exhilarating feeling. There were scheduled fights at different locations against other girl gangs. It did not have to be stated that they could not count on me for physically fighting. They just wanted me to be there and look intimidating. At this point that was a cinch, I had faced so much bullying that the looks of hatred and anger that I gave didn't take much effort on my part.

I got through seventh grade without a scratch and I counted that as a milestone in my life. This must have been my first school year that went by without any mishap. Home life, on the other hand, was getting more and more hostile. I now had the confidence to stand up to my father. That did not fare well, but I wouldn't take his abuse any more. No one in this house barely spoke to one another, everyone had their own demons to fight or didn't care enough to concern themselves with what anyone else must be going through. Ilyse, my youngest sister by ten years, was only six years old and was still spared the insanity thankfully. I hoped she would never have to go through the madness we experienced every day.

The environment was so bad that I could not take the hostility level anymore. I started to plot on just how to get out of there. I had thought of running away several times but was too scared to go through it.

Sherry is my older cousin by nine years. She was a designer of clothing in the garment district. I would get all the samples because I was a size five and she wasn't. Sherry took care of me as best she could like an older sister. Hearing me cry to her day after day, Sherry made me a copy of her apartment key. She was the coolest cousin in the world and I really admired her. She had friends at WBLS, the New York based radio station.

One day I was at Sherry's house with some of her friends, everyone smoking pot and getting really hungry. I felt so grown up when I was with her and her friends. Phoebe Snow was playing in the background, *"Poetry Man."* They took a vote and opted to have Chinese food be delivered. *"Deliver food?? They come to your house???"* I asked, surprised and a bit skeptical thinking that they might be pulling my leg. "Yes", Sherry said and everyone started to laugh. Not at me but with me. I was Sherry's younger cousin, she would not let anyone hurt my feelings.

Before the food arrived, one of the guys pulled out a twenty-dollar bill and told me to run to the corner store on 23rd and 3rd avenue in Chelsea and buy three pints of any kind of Haagen-Dazs I wanted. I couldn't believe it but I flew out the door, and almost peed on myself. I called my mother and told her that I had just spent eleven dollars on ice cream. My mother in her snide way said, *"That's ridiculous, wasting money like that."* I had never tasted anything so creamy and delicious in my life. I was really high!

That year, I was fourteen years old and in eighth grade. I spent most of my time hanging out around the corner at the projects. I met a gangly unattractive boy playing handball and I asked him if I could play. I was a great handball player, yes with the black ball. We became friends like that and used to spend time together, either playing handball or talking. Dominick was kind, gentle and never tried to kiss me. I liked that because deep inside, I was petrified of any boy touching me. I had zero experience with boys. I also knew I was ugly and so was he, so there was no attraction in that way either. We got closer and his single Social Worker mother was crazy about me. It felt a bit weird because I hadn't had any friendship of this type before nor had anyone liked me so much. We hung out at his house and at Bowne Park with my girls and their boyfriends.

I lived so close to my school, the park and the projects that it was encompassing my world. No questions were ever asked about where I was or who I was with. It didn't have anything to do with trust, just the fact that nobody expected anything out of the ordinary from me. My father knew when Dominick would call the house. He screamed that Idi Amin was on the phone only, he would say "DADAAmean." At the time, I didn't know who he was talking about but the message was clear. Dominick and I were together for three years and those three years seemed to pass so quickly, they seemed like a dream. Toward the second year of hanging out, "the kids" at Bowne Park started using drugs. Attending school became so infrequent. I started not being afraid of cutting school. Dominick starting chipping, that is when you go from snorting to shooting in your muscle at the top of your arm. He was progressing quickly, a little too quickly. I once walked in on him in his apartment with Dominick not even noticing me.

He was slumped over enjoying the numbness that creeps in when the heroine rushes through his body. I didn't like it but didn't say anything about it. One day we were hanging out in the local deli, it was getting chilly late in the fall. I was sitting on Dominick's lap when all of a sudden the door to the deli flung open and there stood my father coming so fast toward me I didn't even have a chance to move. He dragged me to the car while I was still in numbing shock at seeing him appear here so unexpectedly.

My mother was sitting in the passenger seat. He threw me in the back seat and turned around to smack me in the face. The barrage of venom was spewing along with his saliva in my face. There was anger and vile disgust on his face. Some neighbor had called my house and said *"your daughter is with this nigger boy"*.

The drugs took over Dominick's life very quickly. He didn't even care who stormed in and grabbed me that day. I was no longer number one in his life. Heroin was his top priority and the thing he lived for, it seemed. We never spoke about the events in our life that had such collateral damage. We just felt safe with one another as there was no expectation and both of us just needed someone. I knew he had plenty of ghosts in his closet but he no longer had the willpower to fight anything or anyone. I didn't probe him about anything which I might find suspicious or disturbing and he didn't ask me about my past.

Six months later, the Bland's most flamboyant and popular homosexual approached me with pictures of him and Dominick in bed holding one another. My head reeled when I saw those images. I was clearly sick to my stomach and thought I would either throw up or faint from the shock. I didn't love him anymore, but I couldn't fathom him being gay.

I imagined all those times spent with him and never suspected anything like this. I had not had experience with anyone but him and now that experience was tainted. I felt disgusted that he had ever touched me and angry at myself for being so naïve as to not see his aloofness as what it really was.

Somehow, I moved on to high school.

Summer 1971

The summer right before tenth grade saw a lot of hanging out and playing "Follow the Leader." The Davis household was typical of many families at Sanford Gardens. The name sounds pleasant enough doesn't it, but it was more like Grey Gardens.

We had a porter that lived in a single room off of the laundry room in one of the back buildings along with a milk machine where you could get a quart for 25 cents. He was tall, wore a green uniform, and had a perpetual hardon on his left side. Everyone saw it, but no one said anything. One day a woman was found in the basement, bludgeoned to death. No one knew who was responsible but Bill, the porter, disappeared shortly after that.

Lori, my sister, and I would play tag with the Caputo brothers who lived there too. We would find tunnels under our building and run through them as fast as we could. Dark creepy spaces filled with spider webs but we didn't mind that. When you are poor, you find the craziest stuff to entertain yourself while your parents are doing their own creepy things. We even made up lots of games which made our imaginations stronger. My father now was participating in daily card games in one of the apartments. We knew whose apartment it was but never knocked on the door. He lost more money than he ever dreamed of making but that didn't stop my father. He didn't have the sense to give it up and none of us could tell him to, nor would he listen to us, so no one bothered. Al had random jobs because he wasn't qualified for anything. He was Smiley's food supermarket detective once in which his job was to watch who stole food and turn them in. Sometimes he used me and Lori as ploys at the cash registers to see if the cashier pocketed any of the money. That was fun but it only lasted a few months. He also worked as a milk man, and was a constant resident at the OTB.

His last job was as a taxi driver. He had anxiously been waiting for Dr. Carlesi, the psychiatrist, to fulfill his end of the deal. Dr. Carlesi would write up reports to the VA and state that my father was so ill that he was to be considered 100% mentally disabled. That came with a check each month and gave us enough money not to worry about eating. It would also give my father more time to laze around and take it out on us, which I dreaded. Yet, still working as a taxi driver, after he got off at one in the morning, he would find a way to gamble away all the money he just earned. He didn't care about his family or his responsibilities. Al was a dreamer, the same one who promised me he would make enough money to buy me a car and an apartment. Speaking truthfully, he was delusional.

He couldn't or didn't want to face reality. He would usually come home in the middle of the night and I always knew when he arrived. I would never sleep soundly enough not to hear that first sound of the key entering the first lock. It made me so anxious for many reasons and I stayed alert until I was satisfied he had gone to sleep. My mother would invariably get out of her bed (Al slept on the couch at this point).

Mom would ask for the money he made and he would start crying which is classic M.O. for manipulation. He used this same thing every single time and I don't know how he thought he could fool anyone with it anymore.

Well, that was wearing very thin for my mom and her disdain for him was very apparent. They rarely spoke at this point and when she had to speak to him, she kept it as short and to the point as possible. It seemed that she was even disgusted by communicating with him. My mother would have done anything to have him leave, she could not bear him. But he would go ballistic at the thought of leaving, he knew he did not have anywhere to go and this was his only refuge. Living on the couch and smoking his cigarettes was as much as anyone could expect from Al Davis and sometimes even that was too much for him.

Government letter in the mail to Al Davis:
100% disability granted!!

It took years and years for this to be finalized.

Tenth Grade

Tenth grade was a whole new world. Long hallways lined with lockers, no more lining up in size places where I was always the last one in line as the tallest girl. You probably had not envisioned me as tall and extremely skinny. I was always particular in what I ate, chicken being one of my favorite foods. Probably it was to get back at my father for hating chicken. I felt good going against him even if it was for such a small thing as this.

"Oh my God, where do I go?" The chaos of the first day was a bit overwhelming, lining up in the gym in alphabetical order. That was better for me because this way at least my name came in handy... Davis. Not bad, no religious or racial connections, just short and sweet. It must have been changed somewhere along the line, because I was sure we couldn't have been fortunate enough to have started off with such a name. Of course, when my parents were asked, neither of them had an answer. No one ever had answers to anything.

I realized when given my schedule in school that I was in all bottom classes. Why was this a surprise to me? I had missed so many days of school that I should have expected this. When you are in these sorts of classes everyone acts out. Kids feel inferior and stupid, and everyone in school is aware of your placements. It makes it worse when others know of your position, it's so embarrassing.

Teachers teach down to their expectations of the population. When you are in the smart class, teachers are proud to be teaching you and speak up to you expecting a certain level of understanding. Kids quickly learn how to behave. Who wouldn't, when they would be taught properly? If you are unteachable and unruly on the other hand, well, you're not worth their time or investment. They don't really bother themselves about you too much and failing became an expectation. The kids in our classes gravitated to each other almost like invisibly holding on to each other for survival. I felt this was because they knew nobody else cared about them and they just had each other to rely on, those who were in the same situation as them were the only ones who could understand them.

Reading was also added to my program. What did they expect from a child that was kept home to comfort her father? No one taught me to read nor did anyone bother to encourage me to read or learn new things. Everything was so hard, I felt like screaming sometimes but I still kept at it. I needed to read it over and over again to try and get the words right. Even then I didn't understand what I was doing. UGH! It was so frustrating. I later found out that I was dyslexic.

My science teacher, Mr. Steven Gaines, was the best! He was the only one who saw something in me. He paid attention to me and genuinely cared about my learning and studies. We were taking an exam once and the girl next to me cheated off my paper. It was obvious when he marked the papers that evening that I wasn't the one who had cheated. He knew it was not me, he told me he could see I was not the type to cheat. I appreciated that at least someone could see something good in me. I really was basically an honest kid except for the identity part.

I signed up for an African dance class, thinking this would be a way to get in with the black girls. They accepted me although I couldn't freakin' dance to anything, no less to the difficult movements of pulsating hips and buttocks. By the way, I did not have one of those either. Ass that is. It would have been great if this had just been an African girls class where I didn't have to dance. I didn't come here to dance anyway, I had come to bond with the black girls. They accepted my story based on my looks. Why wouldn't they? Carol Channing looked white and she was bi-racial.

I went to John Bowne High School on Main Street in Flushing, Queens and was not performing academically at all. The Guidance Counselor recommended Mini School for me which was kind of a lifesaving school. It was in our building behind the cafeteria where all the borderline students were trying to "be saved". There I had the opportunity to have an awesome, young, newly married teacher named Beverly Kasper. We hung out all the time, she was very friendly and made me feel comfortable so that I wasn't embarrassed to make mistakes in front of her. She taught reading and knew I had an inability to interpret what I was reading. She understood me and my situation very well and worked with me to try and overcome it. All the teachers were quite liberal and tried their very best to work with these totally out of the box students. It didn't mean we weren't teachable or completely dumb, it just meant we all were angry and maltreated by those we had as guardians in life. Still not trusting anyone to befriend, I was totally lingering in space. I preferred staying alone rather than being with someone who wouldn't understand me. This went on for another year and a half.

July 22, 1973

That date is my birthdate. No parties, no recognition, no parents to protect me for 17 years. I felt I had already missed out and been deprived of so much that I needed to finally do something drastic. For the last month, I would wander around Main Street Flushing for lack of anything else to do. It was a mundane existence with no direction and no idea of where I wanted to go. In the late 1960's to late 1970's, drug programs were prevalent in urban areas around New York City. They would send out young people to densely populated areas where they would talk and engage people in order to sell raffle tickets to financially support the programs they were representing.

I became friendly with the same boy who was sent out each Saturday morning. I guess he brought back his quota, which was a good thing for me too as I got to meet and talk to him this way. He was my constant friend to meet on Saturday mornings. We would talk about our family problems and he always had the answer. 'Phoenix House'… it's like a family, he told me. They will love you, take care of you and your needs and you get to live there, learn and be productive. At this point I was anything but productive, so it sounded great to me. Coming from my background, something even half this good would be good enough for me. Besides, I liked him a lot! There was one issue though. I had not used drugs other than smoking pot occasionally. How could I go to a therapeutic halfway house when I didn't use drugs? I wondered. I can't remember my friend's name, the one from Main Street. He called the Phoenix House and placed me on the phone. I explained the hellish household I came from and they said they can take me in. Later on, I will describe occurrences in this facility. The only motive they had to take me in was that they collect welfare checks for each body, the more bodies, the better they looked at doing their job.

So, it is the morning of my seventeenth birthday and we arranged that they would pick me up early evening at the same meeting place where my friend and I met each Saturday. I had decided finally to make the move and had reached the point of no return on my decision. When I started packing, Lori started to panic and scream. *"Where are you going??? You can't leave me here alone."* It was truly torture to leave my sister who I had slept next to in our shared high-riser for 15 years of my life. She was the only living person who witnessed what I had lived through, the only one in this house who I felt any kind of bond with. My parents did not try to stop me and I didn't even expect them to. Off I went to 149th Street in the South Bronx. Another red brick building five stories high just like the one I left.

Lori

Lori had been my best and only friend, a bond kept by secrecy. We shared everything and knew everything that happened with us. To tell you the truth, like me, Lori did not fit in either. Chubby, mean and blind as a bat. Her glasses were thicker than coke bottles. The difference between us was that it was very hard to make her do anything she did not want to do, she could be stubborn as a mule, except when it came to me. For me, she would do almost anything. If I told her to do something, she would do it immediately even if she had refused to listen to the same thing from anybody else. She always wanted to be with me and we had never been apart these 15 years. My running away was probably one of the worst memories for her. Lori was like having my own personal alter ego. As I left, the only thing I heard were Lori's desperate cries. "Please don't leave or take me with you" she screamed.

Mommy would literally be pushed to the edge with her behavior. She didn't have the patience to deal with Lori or her attitude. My mom would yell and yell until she became so frustrated to the point of grabbing Lori's hair and dragging her around the living room, or whatever room they happened to be in at the time. "If you don't listen to me, I am going to kill you" she would shout. Lori held steady and barely cried. I absolutely admired that about her. I was the crier. Big time and was not proud of it, but no matter how much I tried to steel myself, it was impossible.

Lori was also very pretty with long straight hair that would be put up in a bun. My father was so proud of her. It was convenient that she resembled his side of the family. At least that saved her from ridicule and abuse. No one saw anyone's beauty because there was so much ugliness around us, namely mine. Glasses were purchased at the VA hospital, hair brushes were sparse, and back then there were no hair products for curly hair. Clothing was purchased at the discount tables at Klein's and Mays. Pants were so short that I was ridiculed for wearing "high waters."

Once, after my father told my mother to do something with "my bush," Mom bought a product named Curl Free. It was so foul to our olfactory senses. I had to hold my nose and both of us coughed through the entire process. My mother, in all likelihood, didn't want to do it, and she was also not the gentlest woman in the world. She pulled and yanked at my thick knotted hair. I admit it was hard, and I let out a cry at every yank. I could never comb it myself. It was a disaster. My hair turned out to be like the hair on the scarecrow from the Wizard of Oz but I was positive I looked worse.

Phoenix House

My first day at Phoenix house was pleasant enough. I was shown to a dormitory style room. It was quite big and was so organized and clean. At home our sink always had spit stains and toothpaste globs everywhere which made me want to throw up in that same sink. We were approximately nine females all sleeping in two very large rooms. All the women were there for their drug use and prostitution which they needed to support their habit. There were sixty-nine men also living on the five floors beneath us and they were there for heroin addiction. It was during the Rockefeller era and lots of money was available to help save the drug addicts.

Did I mention that every one of those human beings was African-American? Poor, angry at the white man, oppressed, desperate, homeless and had just plain hit rock bottom. If you hadn't hit bottom you would not be there. I didn't know what the fuck I was doing there after the honeymoon period ended which was way too soon.

Encounter groups, chores, cleaning and eating was an everyday occurrence and were to be taken seriously. Things needed to shine or they were not clean enough. I found out it was something to do with learning some sort of real responsibility. Encounter groups had around twelve to fifteens residents, all different each time an encounter occurred. We had to endure the harshest, cruelest criticism anyone could endure. Guess who was "beat up" the most. Yup, me. I could be verbally whipped for any reason, but especially for having lied about my race to the outside world. I heard things like "Who could trust you?" No one could ever trust a liar, especially someone who was white and Jewish. It was common belief that Jews manipulated the world with their power and money. No one ever told me about this but I heard it all the time. I wondered where we missed on all that power and money.

As a reality check, I was taken to a barber and had my hair cut so short that all my curls were gone. No more biracial girl. Just one really frightened, fucked up Jewish girl. I tended to need affection, not the sexual kind, but the kind that had been withheld from me my whole life. I felt neglected from the affection which other children took for

67

granted. Stroking meant you are a good girl, sort of like stroking your dog that just lays there next to you. In Phoenix House, after months of earning trust, sometimes you can touch each other. One day, during a lazy Sunday, I was playing with this guy's hair. The following Monday, I was blasted during encounter group for stroking his hair. They told me that white people would get lucky if they stroked a black man's head. *"Is that what you were doing, Randi?"* I had not ever heard of such silliness in my life. It did not matter, no one believed anything I said. It wasn't anything new for me.

Four months along, my Grandfather Harry died and because he was not my biological grandfather, I was not granted permission to attend the funeral. I didn't care much except that I couldn't go out for the day. There was hardly any chance of going out of the house, my friend from Main Street had truly been lucky that he was sent out every week, even if it was for work.

The following week however, I was promoted to a job only entrusted to someone who has earned time under their belt. My new job was a really important one and I felt worthwhile. I would go each Sunday morning around 4 a.m., escorted by two of our largest male residents for safety of course, to Hunts Point Market. The job title was acquisition and my job was to go to each vendor and ask them for donations. As soon as we arrived at the market, my adrenaline would rise. My boots would hit the ground sliding through the melted ice that kept the fish fresh. The vendors started to know me and were even nice to me, putting boxes away for us to take. I was so successful I was actually acknowledged at family meetings. That was big as it wasn't easy to get this position. With my sweet white face, I was able to achieve exactly what the administration intended and which would have been difficult for the others. The sound and smells were so different in the middle of a winter night. I was chilled to the bone but filled with the warmth of anticipation that I was going to get it done! Only Randi could do this job well! I was successful and I knew this. I was so happy once for a change!!!

There was a guy at Phoenix House who was not typical at all, sort of like me. He was attending Harvard. He lived in Connecticut and was from a very wealthy family. In those days people like him were referred to as "high yella" people. Very fair skinned with grey eyes. As expected, he was given a hard time also. Rich boy, "high yella" and never did a day in prison. We gravitated toward each other as our situation made us relate to each other. Looks would have different meanings and we both understood them without having to use words. He was convicted because he was selling high quantities of cocaine to Harvard students. A crime that definitely would get you some penitentiary time. However, mom and dad had enough money for a really good defense team and hence, he landed at Phoenix House. He was absolutely stuck there or else he was to pass Go and go directly to jail. So, obviously, he preferred staying here.

I was getting tired of getting up in the bitter cold, walking around begging for food. I would get comments from the vendors like *"what is a girl like you doing with your life?"* I hadn't a clue. What was I going to do and what was I doing right now?

One of my roommates was getting tired also. She was a lesbian and her parents rejected her, so she embraced drugs to kill the pain of being rejected by her family. She was the only female of four siblings. She was in there longer than me by months. She earned enough privileges to

70

be trusted so that she could jog each morning before any one was up. A night man would check on all sleeping residents every twenty minutes. His flashlight peered into our faces. Had to be sure no one split from the house. Many goings on there were illegal. In those days, the founders of therapeutic communities convinced those who were funding the programs that addicts had to be treated harshly with firm and consistent punishment. Flexibility was not an option.

My "friend" with more privileges decided we would create a plan to escape. We both wanted to leave. Let me make myself very clear. Although I had not committed any crime or used any drugs, I still couldn't leave. I was placed in a room with one of the clinical directors for a few hours' time for him to brainwash me into believing that I had to remain there or I would fall back into my old patterns of destructiveness. They called my house once to tell them I was unhappy and wanted to leave. They completely manipulated their words to convince my parents that it was in everyone's best interest that I stay in treatment. My mother was the first to completely agree. In my mother's eyes, I was the identified problem in this household and as long as I am not present my father had no one to overtly hate. Therefore, no fighting. No one could see or even try to understand my side or what I actually went through.

One month later, six months into my imprisonment, my friend and I plotted just how we would escape. We were determined to leave. We would be as quiet as church mice, put on sweats to go to sleep (it was January) and when the night man finished his rounds, we would run as fast as we could, open the fire escape door to the roof (which had an alarm) and jump to the connecting building. We did it, we actually did it. We ran and ran all the way to a main street where we were able to find a pay phone. I called my father collect and he accepted the charges. He answered, *"Hi Cookie, do you want to come home?"* I knew he loved me.

He got in his Pontiac and came and got us. There was no us by the time he got there. My "friend" couldn't do it. I begged her not to return. The punishment would be huge! I guess she returned. I never saw her again.

Daddy took me back home.

Home Sweet......

Daddy picked me up on a random corner.

Blissfully, we embraced each other. We arrived home at around five in the morning. I was met by my extremely anxious mother and my sister who was so deeply hurt that she could not even look at me. Lori ended up not speaking to me for more than a month. She was good at holding grudges and did it extremely well. She had inherited that trait straight from my mother and the deal was that once you messed with her it was never forgotten, let alone forgiven.

In two weeks, it was going to be Lori's turn to be the center of attention at her very own low-budget sweet sixteenth birthday. You know, the kind with the red checkered table cloths and the tray of yesterday's leftover pasta that is smothered in some sort of sauce so you couldn't tell what's under there. It seemed as if I had come home to cast a shadow over her one and only chance to be the center of attention.

Every moment was filled with the possibility that someone from Phoenix House was going to walk in and take me back to fix all my psychological problems. It was a perfect way to catch me off guard and no one would have objected except for my dad. My father's ally, Dr. Carlesi, was paid to attend any event that was too much for my dad to handle alone. It was not a frequent occurrence, however. If we counted, do you know how many times there were in total that we celebrated anything in our lives? Twice, to be exact. All things happy were turned into such a procedure with the constant worry of whether or not daddy could get Dr. Carlesi to come with him. He was a no-show to everyone's graduation ceremony. Grandma Yetta, then, was our seat filler.

There was one call from Phoenix House to explain why I should be brought back, but dad stood firm and fought with my mother to keep me home. Dad even called her a cold bitch!

Every day I woke up worse than the day before. The girl who weighed one hundred and seventeen pounds before running away from home was now gorging herself on everything she could find. Nothing filled me up. My father allowed me to lay in bed as long as I wanted. At least I was not hanging out with any "niggers." Forty pounds later and very depressed, I contemplated what was going to happen to me. I had no education, no aspirations and no clue about anything.

Sometime during my first month home, my father had another breakdown. Back he went to his favorite safe haven, the VA hospital. This time, though, it was different. After two weeks had passed, my mother was asked to come in with me and my sister Lori; Ilyse was too young. This was the seventies and family counseling was in the beginning stages then. My mom agreed to see this young new Social Worker.

We reluctantly piled into the car and drove down the Belt Parkway to Fort Hamilton. The trucks zoomed by us making so much noise. I had not experienced this journey before. I was the only one to have never visited this loony bin. I was scared of what I was going to see. Truth be told, when my father was in an agitated state and I did not comfort him, he became so angry he would scream out of desperation: *"You are going to land up in the same crazy hospital somewhere sucking your thumb!"* I still sucked my thumb! I was terrified this was a ploy to get me admitted to the hospital.

Mr. Sidney Kleinman

We were told to ride the yellow elevator to the sixth floor. It was worse than expected and we could hear the screams even before the locked metal door rang us in! My mother and Lori were already crying really hard. Snot was running down Lori's face. There were no tissues! I was not crying. My wall was strong and proud. This asshole was not going to see my weakness.

We were greeted by a youngish man. I was not looking at anyone directly. We were told to have a seat, and my father was brought in from the locked unit. He walked in wearing a worn light blue cover up, the ones that tie in the back. Thank God, he was wearing something

77

underneath. I had seen enough of his pink penis in my life. We sat there as my father cried, which wasn't anything new. It turned out that Mr. Kleinman had asked us to come in to explain that he had been working with my father and the only way our problems could be resolved was if we all worked together.

The room had no windows and we were surrounded by these ugly ass concrete walls. I was not going to cry or talk, no matter what. This was their problem, not mine. I was not the crazy one here, they were. However, that was not explained to him in that way at all. It was I who was presented as the problem and the cause of all the conflict in our household. I am not sure how long this went on. It felt like forever. The smell of institutional food and sweaty men was pervasive and overwhelming. When this meeting ended, I think our new and enthusiastic Mr. Kleinman saw what kind of shit he had gotten himself into. He asked my parents to step outside. I think they were the ones who had to step outside due to safety restrictions of the hospital. Our Mr. Kleinman suggested that he see me in his private office free of charge.

My father and mother were now in couples counseling and I was taking the train to the richest, whitest neighborhood I had ever been in for therapy. Right next to his building was a fancy pastry shop. Pastries were and are my favorite things to eat. I guess they reminded me of a better version of Devil Dogs. Every week, I would get on the 7-train, switch to the number 6, and get off at 36th street. His office was at 34th and Park Ave. Could you imagine me going to a Park Ave office? I never forgot to go to the pastry store as a reward after my session with this nerd was over. We sat there week after week with me not saying a word. The fifty minutes were endless. That did not matter to him. He would repeat the same words each week: *"We will sit here until you accept the fact that I am not going to touch you in any way."* How did he know? Each week, I wore a black turtleneck to protect my body, at least unconsciously. Approximately, a month passed before we first began discussing what I thought my first step should be in making my life better. He gently approached the idea of going to a GED program to get a high school diploma. After all, what was I going to do without an education? I listened to him and, after a while, became less guarded with him.

Sisters

Our family was so divided and triangulated. All members were ready with knife in hand to retaliate. Since I gave my father all he needed to cut me out of his life, now there were only two daughters left in his life. He was so good at this game. He would slip money to one of my sisters and say to her, *"Don't tell your sister I gave this to you"*. Then he would take the other one out to dinner and direct her not to tell the other. The lies and the set-ups for betrayal were like a minefield filled with live ammunition. No matter where my sisters stepped, they did not realize there was a chance that a limb would be lost. There were, after all, ramifications for everything.

Of course, every time they saw my father or received seed money, one of them told my mother. My mother never missed out on the chance to inform me of my sister's acceptance of his briberies. That led to more jealousy and resentment. My mother was not aware that by telling me of their actions, she made me feel like she couldn't be trusted either. Her motive was to keep me close and loyal to her, as she had been doing since I was a little girl. My mother's constant reminder was, *"You know you've always been my favorite daughter."*

Flushing High School GED Program

What am I doing here? This was yet another place where I felt that I did not belong. Everyone was scruffy and uninterested. Again, the teachers had the attitude that they had to be there in order to work with the losers. For the test, everyone had to bring two number two pencils and skip the seat next to them. I had to sit there for six straight hours. Language Arts, Reading, Social Studies, Math and Science. Forty-five minutes for each part. Bathroom breaks in between.

Honestly, I had absolutely no interest in passing this exam, at least that's what I told myself. Stakes were way too high to really study and then fail and face Mr. Kleinman. See, I am not smart or pretty or valuable in anyway. I told him that but it was not a good enough answer for him. *"I guess you are just going to take it until you pass,"* he used to say to me. Second, third, fourth and fifth time I went back to that hot classroom. I hated it!

Why must I pass this? What was the point? *"This is not going to make my life any better,"* I would say to Mr. Kleinman. *"You must build one block at a time,"* he would respond.

I was moping on my bed after five failure notices when one day, my mother came in and tossed an envelope on my bed. It was a larger envelope this time. Never putting two and two together in my brain, I was just preparing myself for another failure letter. It wasn't! Never would I have believed for one single moment that passing that test would bring me so much joy. I didn't even want to take it in the first place. Tears streamed down my face harder than I could remember in quite a long time. These were definitely happy tears. WOW! This was amazing; passing something brought a new feeling of achievement to me. I did not care if my parents thought it was a big deal or not. I knew Mr. Kleinman did. That is all that mattered from here on in to me. All of a sudden, I realized how cute he was. *"Could he marry me now?"* Maybe not this moment but later when I proved some more things to him.

The following week, I walked into his office and saw his leg in a cast from knee down. *"What happened?"* I asked him. He said he broke his leg skiing. Secretly I thought, did he know what a great caretaker I was. I could fix a simple broken leg, no problem. I had to fix way bigger things in my life. Months of therapy for me continued and slowly I trusted him more and more. He had not touched me yet. Next goal to be worked on was to find employment with my newly earned GED. Time to pay for my sessions. No more freebees. I was a competent woman now at 19 years old.

Al Moves Out

My parents finally came to the conclusion that they were better off separated from each other than together. I had never known my father to have even a thimble of self-confidence before. Kleinman was a miracle therapist, indeed! Dad moved out into a neighborhood called Rosedale to a small apartment. His familiar smell followed him there, too. My mother was jumping for joy. Who could blame her, she had just lost 165 pounds of burden.

Booth Memorial Hospital

My mother was now 41 years old. She went to
her gynecologist one day because she felt a lump in her
breast. He examined her and sent her on her way, telling
her that there was nothing to worry about. This doctor
definitely made her feel like she didn't deserve any
compassion. Six months later the lump had grown bigger.
Mom called and made another appointment.

Mommy came home that day and told me that, as
the oldest daughter, I had to be brave because she needed to
have an operation. No! I couldn't live without this woman.
I hadn't achieved what I needed yet. Besides, there were
two more kids at home. One was seventeen and the other
was nine. How was I to support them? Shit always happens
to us.

Lori and I sat in the waiting room in a state of
denial. I prayed to...someone. Who? I have no idea. But
pray I did and as hard as I could. *"Please God, I need her.
We all need her."* I couldn't possibly raise the girls, and

one thing I knew for sure was that my father would definitely not step up to the plate. He was not even there to support his terrified daughters emotionally. What would we do for money? The doctors spoke to us just as they wheeled my mother up to the operating room. They said that if nothing happened they would come down and find us in about an hour. One, two, three and then four hours passed. I sat there still, reassuring myself and my sister Lori that our mother would be fine and that they were just taking longer than they were supposed to. The automatic sliding doors opened and closed and people huddled in their own support systems. Overflowing garbage bins and half-finished coffee containers surrounded the waiting area.

Whispering, crying, uneven and distressed breathing could be heard intermittently. Those plastic seats we sat in for so long offered little comfort to our bodies. My sister and I held hands while continually fidgeting around in our chairs.

Then, some familiar faces walked toward me and as I was the eldest, they started to explain the medical mumbo jumbo to me. Was I supposed to know what this meant? My olfactory senses were strong as they always were. The antiseptic or disinfectant was very sharp and someone had just vomited. I guess their news was not good either. The team of my mom's surgeons walked over with tissues in hand and explained that she had stage three breast cancer and one of her three main lymph nodes were positive. My mom would have to endure chemotherapy and rounds of radiation. I stayed by her side until she was released from the hospital. I learned how to empty her drains and I took her to every chemo appointment.

Healing Karen

After a couple of months, my mom bounced back. Nothing stopped this woman. She had to return to work as a librarian on Wall Street, filing and storing microfiche for an investment company. Mom really was doing well. She did, however, look like Pope John Paul with her head bald and her body bloated from the chemo. Her employer was really good to her. They got taxis to take her home at night when they knew she was tired and had no money left. To go on the subways and take two trains and then proceed to walk eight blocks before she reached home was too much for her.

Back to Therapy

Now that it appeared that mommy was doing okay, it was time for me to go back to Mr. Kleinman and work on getting a job and on many more issues. There were no jobs out there for an unskilled nineteen-year old.

I sabotaged myself to avoid making strides in my life. It was going to take a bit more patience for Mr. Kleinman and a little less resistance from me to bring in some results. I wasn't sure if I was quite there yet.

I worked hard in therapy and we came up with a tentative plan. I would join the Peace Corps and see how other people lived and maybe acquire some skills that would help me get some work when I returned. I went to the office of the Peace Corps and filled out the paper work. After a while I was sent options of what countries might be of interest to me.

I realized that I was scared shitless to leave what was familiar to me. I had always felt unsafe at home, in my neighborhood, and at school. Leaving the country would be way beyond my comfort zone. There was one little legal matter, though. I had already signed on the dotted line. I met with a counselor and explained just how terrified I was to leave my safety net; besides, my mom was still battling breast cancer. This woman was very nice and explained to me that I must fulfill my responsibility since I had already made a commitment.

She asked me how working at Riker's Island Prison sounded to me. My position would be to counsel adolescent boys six months prior to their release. It sounded great! I wouldn't have to leave Queens and I would have a stipend so I could also afford my twenty-five dollar fee for therapy. The main office was in the Bronx and now, instead of it being called Peace Corps, it was called VISTA, "Volunteers in Service to America".

This was a perfect environment for me. Every one of the counselors was African-American and the supervisor was happy he was getting a Caucasian counselor. I felt really important. I had to get fingerprinted, wait for clearance, and wear a certain standard of dress code. The overall year went well. I earned my completion certificate and was now able to look for jobs. That year gave me a lot of confidence going forward. Working at a prison was not easy. Everywhere you walked, a corrections officer followed you. We were also locked up behind those gates. Not a comfy feeling, let me tell you. There were, however, some valuable lessons taught by trained Social Workers who trained us to conduct group therapy sessions. The boys sought me out because they trusted me and needed to talk. I was one of nine female counselors. It was not only that they wanted to be around females. They couldn't talk to their cohorts in prison because that would make them look like "pussies." So they came to me to talk and I helped them out in the ways that I could. For the first time in perhaps ever, I felt a deep sense of accomplishment.

Dr. Daniel Casriel

It was time for me to look for real employment. I was informed by a former colleague that there was this psychiatrist who trained you for a year, and if you completed the program, you would be given a job at one of his two therapeutic houses. This was a very big opportunity. Dr. Casriel was the founding father of Daytop Village. He was a man of distinction. He had written a book in 1972 called "A Scream Away from Happiness." In the late 1960's, he had extended his practice to include a small therapeutic community program called AREBA, short for Accelerated Re-Education of the Emotions, Behavior and Attitudes. Dr. Casriel's office was in a very affluent neighborhood in midtown Manhattan. He wanted to attract elite clientele. Children of famous people were admitted for treatment there. I did my training in Manhattan and went through everything their clients went through.

Intense emotional therapy was a true understatement. We attended groups every day and had to be willing to bare our souls. We, as trainees, worked very close together as each and every waking minute was spent there. I had never allowed myself to feel such closeness with anyone before. Dr. Casriel ran most groups and strictly observed whether you were working hard enough or not. The work consisted of talking and screaming. When a person would talk about something painful, Dr. Casriel would then advise you to begin to scream and to scream till you began to cry. It was his belief that this treatment was most effective in getting rid of your pain. It did feel very cathartic and freeing. Someone in the group would always physically hold you through this process. You never felt alone in shedding your pain. This was entirely different than I had felt at Phoenix House. I actually felt safe in the therapeutic house. So, I worked very hard not just for myself but for him as well. I would think to myself, *"Think what you could be if you learned this process from a very skilled psychiatrist!"*

I completed my tenure and obtained employment in his facility located in Morristown, New Jersey. The schedule there was to work four days straight and then go home for three. I was back in Flushing living with my mom and my two sisters. I purchased my first car for nine hundred dollars, a green Fiat. That car got me back and forth and lasted longer than I could have expected.

The New Jersey facility was filled with foster kids: angry, violent and with minimal luxuries if you compared them to the Manhattan facility. Dr. Casriel promised that if I paid my dues there and created some change, I could return to Manhattan. And I did. I was starting to feel different about myself. My clothing style was taking on a new look. I carried myself with more confidence. Maybe it works in the opposite way. You gain some confidence and then you start carrying yourself like you matter. It was now okay for me to be seen by others!

The staff in the Manhattan facility was worked to death, however. We worked approximately 70-hour weeks. Each week you had to man the house overnight and dispense meds. This went on for about a year. I was beginning to get burnt out.

It was time for me to move on.

Therapy

I was still sporadically seeing Mr. Kleinman. I believe he was proud of my hard work. There was still a lot of emotional work to be done. I still needed to work on intimacy with men and closeness with women. I had not yet created any significant friendships. It was a hard process, working through so many layers of issues.

When we were kids, Lori and I never knew where to begin the cleaning process in our room. There wasn't enough room to make a significant change in how the roomed appeared. It's not much different in your physical body, if you think about it. After all, how much pain can be shifted from one place to another before change starts to show?

First Female....

There was an ad in the New York Times employment section looking for a counselor to work in a medium security prison in Staten Island. The name was Arthur Kill Correctional Facility.. It opened in 1976 with 931 inmates. It was located right next to a major landfill for garbage. Thousands of birds hovered all over the garbage. The stench in the summer was unbearable.

I had learned how to represent myself very well, and I convinced them that I had enough knowledge to do the job. I still had a very tough veneer. I looked like I could handle the position. There were still not a lot of opportunities for someone in the counseling field without formal education. I went through many interviews with the corporation's director, Mr. Ron Williams. He was in charge of funding the counseling program for the inmates. The program (still in existence) is called "Stayn' Out" prison project.

The job paid ten thousand dollars a year! I had finally made it. Not only did I get the job, I was the first female who was not a correctional officer hired to counsel male prisoners. I was given extensive orientation in the way things had to be expressed and the manner in which they had to be handled. My clothing should not, in away way, be open to being interpreted as seductive and I was to stay at a distance of at least six feet from the inmates at all times.

Doing cartwheels and back flips for my attention were the five male counselors. I worked with the prisoners and they respected me and didn't do anything to jeopardize our sessions. Corrections officers were a different breed altogether. They were worse than the prisoners.

The male staff was really protective of me, however. I had my own personal correction guard moving with me like Peter Pan's shadow. Never for one second was I unaccompanied, unless I was using the bathroom. In that case, he stood outside till I was done. It was quite a lot to handle, being behind so many locked gates. All the counselors working at "Stayn' Out" were recovering

98

addicts. But I was not aware of that information then. I couldn't tell either; after all, I wasn't one.

I still had my trusty Fiat that took me each day on those torturous beat up roads, first the Grand Central Parkway, then the Belt Parkway, and then over the Verrazano Bridge to Staten Island. The trucks filled the air with fumes as thick as clouds. Sometimes I could see or inhale them. But I was making 10,000 dollars a year and that was enough to keep me there.

Mr. Billy Watson

One of my colleagues asked me for a ride back

to Flushing so he could pick up the subway to Manhattan where he lived. He said that he would pay me for my weekly gas. I happily agreed. At the beginning, it was a bit awkward. He was not really loquacious. He was a very quiet and a very smart man. I liked our conversations a lot. Intellect was my turn on. The fact that he did not try anything sexual with me also scored him big points. A month went by and one day, on my car seat I saw a large, circular, multi-colored lollipop that looked like it was purchased from Coney Island. A card was attached to it. It was so romantic! I can't remember exactly what the words were and I did not even keep the card, but I can recall that it went something like this: *"You make me feel as vibrant as the colors on this lollipop. Would you consider going out to dinner with me?"*

I immediately said yes. Our drives back and forth to work were never the same again. The sexual tension was palpable. We kissed and fondled each other for weeks. The day finally arrived when Billy told me something that would forever change my life!

He began to cry and told me this God-awful story about how he was raised in High Point, North Carolina by his aunt. When he was a small boy, he was rough-housing with his cousins in the back yard of his aunt's house. That is where a large black cast iron cauldron was kept to do the laundry. The water was at the boiling stages when his cousin ran into him and Billy was tossed into the boiling water. Everyone ran for help but the damage was done. For many weeks after that, Billy had to rest with just a netting over him so that mosquitos couldn't get to him.

He stayed in a dilapidated hospital in the segregated south for more than a year. No technology, no advanced pain medication was available at that time. He was unconscious for most of the year. He could not be moved to New York to where his biological parents lived until he was stable enough to be transported by ambulance. Billy suffered severe burns over three quarters of his body. Skin graft after skin graft was done but the burns were so bad that even this did not help him.

Eunice and Charles Watson

When Billy was brought to a burn unit in New York City, it was there that he met his parents for the very first time. Charles, Billy's father, came from a highly educated family. All Charles' siblings were college educated. His niece taught at Duke University. When he married, Eunice, an uneducated woman, his family could not hide their disappointment in him.

Charles was a very mean man. Every night upon arriving home, Charles picked up a bottle of whiskey. The more he drank, the more violent be became. He did not want children, so when Eunice conceived Billy, he was sent immediately to her family in North Carolina to be raised.

Now that Billy had been returned to New York for extended care for his burns, Charles resented him even more. Billy was finally released with skin that felt like layers of leather piled on top of each other. His skin was webbed under both arms. The melted skin would forever be a reminder of that fateful day.

Billy was now not only tortured by his deformity, but by his father's insanity. He was not allowed to watch television when he came home from school even though both his parents worked all day. Charles would plant a wedge of paper as a trap. If Billy watched TV and the paper was moved, he would be given a beating.

However, it was clear from the beginning that everyone recognized Billy's intelligence. He read extensively and his vocabulary was impressive. Billy graduated Valedictorian from high school and was accepted to Duke University. While in high school, Billy met a girl, and had three daughters with her without ever telling his parents. He was sixteen years old when his first daughter was born. Her first Easter, he dressed his daughter up to present her as his proudest achievement to his parents, but he was stopped in his tracks. When he rang the doorbell, his mother opened the door and before Billy was able to say anything, she shouted, *"I never want to see that whore's daughter again."* That day was another horrific day in Billy's life. His parents never saw any of his children.

Billy went off to Duke just as his parents had hoped. As time went, on his peers noticed his odd behavior when he was drunk. He would cry uncontrollably and ask, "Why me?" He even became violent to those around him.

Randi and Billy

I was twenty when my relationship with Billy began. The day Billy shared that he had something awful to tell me was the day many things became clear to me. Now I knew why there were never any sexual advances. He thought I would reject him and be horrified by the feel of his skin. I interpreted this as a good thing. Somehow, I thought he knew I wanted it that way. Slow and steady, with no fast moves.

The day finally arrived that we decided to trust one another and be intimate, with an unspoken promise that we would not hurt each other. I was even more horrified than he could have imagined. What my fingers were feeling was unimaginable. My first instinct was to pull away. But how could I do this to him? After all, this was the reason why he had not confided in me for so long a time.

I did not have what it takes to hurt someone so deeply. I got used to the textures, the way his skin almost felt like wave prints in hardened sand. I was not even sure if he could feel sensation. The extreme heat was dreadful for Billy because it prevented him from socializing. When everyone else was dressed in light summer clothes he would wear long pants and long sleeves. From his neck down, the skin was damaged. Above his neck he had one ear that was fused to his head. I had not given it a lot a lot thought before I learned his complete story. Despite everything he had endured, he was very sweet, thoughtful and romantic.

When I confided to him about my mother's diagnosis and my fears of not being able to take care of my sisters financially, Billy immediately said that it was not a problem. He suggested that, if need be, we could all move in together and that he would help me care for them. Too much was happening too quickly. I still needed to sort things out. It appeared that he was the immediate answer to the complex issues of my life. I was so scared to be alone! It's ironic, now that I think back. I had always been alone, I just had never realized it.

I had no idea about Billy's alter ego! That was his side that abused alcohol. He hid his alcohol intake from me but I found out that he drank every day before he got home from work. He would say, *"I went out for a drink with the guys."* Except, there were never really any guys. There was just this one very isolated and damaged man. Mental illness almost always mimics the same behaviors as alcoholism; it leaves the children of both feeling like life is unpredictable. Children are left with emotional and behavioral problems due to the chaos that surrounds them. That is all that I had ever known. What I didn't know then was that we repeat what we have experienced in our lives. I had not had enough therapeutic intervention to recognize this pattern. Just like my father, Billy loved me in all the wrong ways. I did not know how to recognize a healthy relationship. I had never seen or been in one.

I never doubted his love, ever. He treated me as the most beautiful woman in the world. He would always walk with me with his chest puffed out like the proudest peacock. He was generous beyond his own means. Billy was only making twelve thousand dollars a year, but supported me all the way through undergraduate and graduate school without a single complaint.

Nothing is Ever Free

Billy and I lived together for four years before we were married. I needed to wait for my grandmother to die. If she knew her prized Jewish granddaughter was marrying a black man twelve years her senior, she would have died a lot sooner.

I must confess that I didn't want to marry him. It's not that I did not love him. The truth is that mere love is not enough. Billy had given me bruises as a result of his drinking. He humiliated me by walking into one of my college classrooms to check on me. His behavior was erratic and unpredictable, just like my father's had been.

Earlier, Billy had bought me this beautiful Main Coon kitten. He was gorgeous. Billy named him Captain Bo. Every time Billy would get drunk the same pattern repeated itself. First, he would cry and ask me how I could love a deformed man. No matter how much I reassured him, he switched on and off just like a light bulb. He became enraged because he thought that I was lying. Next came the choking and the pushing and when things really got out of hand, he would pick up my cat by his neck and threaten to kill him in front of me. This made me even more terrified. I would cry and beg him to not hurt my cat. When he was a small boy, I knew he had to kill chickens for dinner. So I knew he had the capacity to easily kill my cat. I'm relieved that he never did it though he threatened to more times than I can count.

After two years of working in another counseling drug program, I decided that this was bullshit. Why should the personnel take advantage of my innate counseling skills and pay me next to nothing? I decided to take this issue up with Billy. I explained that I wanted to go to college. I would be the first "Davis" to ever graduate from college. As always, when Billy was in his normal state, he would never say no to me. We both understood it was going to be a real financial strain, but it would be well worth it.

Formal Education

I applied to York College and received all the financial aid I could get. I also applied to the "SEEK" program, which allocates money for text books and gives underachieving students extra academic assistance. I loved it there! We received a personal counselor for any sort of support we needed. I felt like we were a beautifully woven blanket made up of the most diverse cultures and colors. That was the prevalent feeling among many in the student body. Many of us were nontraditional learners. In the CUNY system, York was not highly rated. However, the college had a special ability to recognize talent in students with low GPA's in high school. Most of us did not have parental support, either financially or in understanding the role of education in attaining success.

Within a few months in the academic environment, I became an avid learner. I studied all day and earned all A's. I made the Dean's List every semester without fail. This was so surreal for me. I still had not gained confidence in my abilities. I attended classes each summer and in between semesters for extra credit. This was now a mission! Nobody for any reason was going to stop me from learning.

I began my first semester at York in February. In my second year, my counselor and I started exploring graduate schools. However, it became apparent that all graduate schools began in September. This meant I would have to wait a whole six months to enroll or graduate in three and half years. I chose to work my ass off and take twenty-four credits in my last semester. It became too difficult and I was failing my computer class. I just couldn't understand the programming aspect at all. The pressure was insurmountable. I begged the teacher for some consideration and explained that I had already gotten into graduate school for a dual degree in Family and Marriage Counseling and School Counseling. At this point, I was headed for graduation with a 3.7 GPA.

This young hippie of a teacher thought I was trying to get away without doing what was expected of me. He would not budge one fucking inch. I had to go to the Dean of Students and explain that if I did not pass this class, I would not only not graduate but also not go to graduate school at Queens College.

Thank God, I was given a "D" in the class and graduated Cum Laude instead of Summa Cum Laude.

As much passion and drive as I had during those three and a half years at York, something other than the thirst for knowledge was driving me. It was my desire to get out of everything I had experienced personally.

I earned two degrees in college. In hindsight, I have no fucking clue how I did this. Life could have been so beautiful if Billy just stopped drinking. One hot summer day, I was in class in summer school and the door opened wildly and to my humiliation, it was Billy. He came in drunk, staggering and slurring his words, looking for his wife, and everyone looked at each other in bewilderment. He couldn't find me in the midst of all the other students. I just got up quietly and left the classroom. It took so much strength to walk into class the following day and have everyone stare at me. But I knew that Billy was not going to stop me from completing that four-credit class.

Millions of people in relationships with addicts or abusive people think they are omnipotent; they think they can change another human being. I tried everything, threatening him that I would leave him if he didn't go to AA or counseling but he would never commit. Despite those threats, I didn't leave him. Not yet, at least.

Twenty-Nine Years Old

I was in counseling with a psychiatrist because my panic attacks had come back with a vengeance. It was my last year of graduate school. I was graduating with a 3.4 GPA. I had recently been in a car accident. I was fine physically but this incident triggered a new set of panic attacks. I really needed to think about what I wanted to do with the rest of my life. I had been with Billy for nine years. I did know one thing for certain. He was never going to stop his abusive behavior, not even for the person he claimed to love more than anyone else.

I was working hard in therapy and contemplated having a baby. I made one last ditch attempt at motivating Billy to give up drinking. Then, toward the middle of July, I got pregnant. It was a couple of months after graduation.

Billy's drinking became worse. How can this be? My therapist explained to me that he was dependent on me, but now I was more focused on my pregnancy rather than on him.

The pregnancy was very hard. In my sixth month, I contracted a UTI (urinary tract infection) which made me very weak. I called my obstetrician, but he dismissed it as nothing. As usual, Billy was intoxicated. I asked him to bring me the thermometer. My temperature was 104 degrees. I had to let him drive me to Long Island Jewish Hospital, to the emergency room. I felt so ashamed of myself. Even that sick, I was so aware and concerned about how the staff at the hospital looked at me. I knew I was going to be treated without respect or sympathy.

It was 1986 and a white woman was walking into the emergency room with her very drunk black husband. You can imagine how people saw me then. I was immediately placed on an ice bed to bring down the fever. I was given antibiotics but I was scared out of my mind. My husband was not lucid enough to take care of me. My mother wasn't available either. She was out with men and had instructed me to never interrupt her when she was "socializing". After two days in the hospital, I was released but was placed on bed rest for the rest of my pregnancy. Billy went to work and during the day I could relax a little until I heard that very familiar sound of the key turning.

The script never changed. My father or Billy, it was the same feeling of dread.

Three months later, at 37 weeks, I went into labor. I was alone in the hospital room, pushing and pushing but not progressing at all. Twelve hours later, they gave me Pitocin and I had to push for four more hours. The doctor had not been nice to me since the day he met my black husband, smelling of stale day-old alcohol that permeated throughout all his pores, like gasoline at the gas station. I despise that odor to this day. I refused an epidural and the doctor yelled at me for not pushing hard enough. I guess he had more important stuff to do besides delivering a biracial baby.

Ashley was born March 22, 1986. So was I!

I was done with Billy, but now I had to accumulate enough courage to execute the plan. My life was now all about raising my daughter. No one was ever going to lay their hands on her. I made sure of this by never letting her be out of my sight. I breastfed her for two and a half years. I was so in love with this baby that nothing else mattered but her. Ashley's breath was a sweet smell of mother's milk. I would place my nose by her mouth and inhale deeply to calm myself so I could get through another day of angst.

Chanukah

Ash was now three years old and starting to show signs of stress. I was not going to close my eyes to anything, no matter how hard this was going to be. Billy was still working but money was very tight. I went to IKEA to buy Ash her first desk as a Chanukah gift. The following day I asked Billy to please put the desk together. Bad move on my part, to ask him to do this on a Saturday morning when he had a hangover. Billy got frustrated easily and could not tolerate any expectations at that point, mine or anyone else's. He had lost his wife to this baby girl. His rage manifested itself because Ashley started to have a tantrum. She was so bright and wanted her desk put together now!

Billy was enraged and slapped Ashley across her face. This was the first and the last time he did that. He left his hand print on her cheek. I was like a circuit breaker that "trips" off the electrical flow to protect the circuit from overheating. I did not even take a second to think. I was done. I slept with Ashley in my arms in her bed holding on to her for dear life. I never closed my eyes. I did not care what he did to me. However, seeing him strike her made me visualize what her life was going to be like if I stayed with him. Was I going to allow her to experience a life like mine? Absolutely not. I was not taking the path my mother took, making excuses and ruining the way my baby views herself and will do so in all relationships to come.

That day was the last day of my marriage.

Ash and I

I work fast when my mind is made up. That week, I started looking for an apartment close to where we were living. Fortunately, I found an apartment for not a lot of money across the street from Queens College. I arranged for the lease to be placed in Billy's name, and gathered the essentials for Billy to live comfortably. He would never have done this for himself. When it was ready, I drove him there and explained how he was less than two miles from me and I would help him adjust to his new life. He had to accept that our relationship was over.

By now, I had applied and gotten a job with the Board of Education as a drug counselor. It was perfect. I enrolled Ashley into a pre-school (the director was a colleague of mine in graduate school). This was one of the best schools in the area, The UN International School, off the Long Island Expressway in Queens. It was easily accessible to me no matter where I was assigned. This was still very scary for me. I had never left Ash alone with anyone, including my mother. But I could trust Lydia, the director. She knew my history to some extent. Yet, still it was hard for me and Ash. When I would drop her off, she would scream *"Don't leave me!"* Her teacher was a gentle young woman of maybe twenty-five years. She is at the stage of life when you have a generous amount of patience. Ashley's teacher had more patience than a gardener tending to her roses. Ashley began to love school. It was safe and she made friends; her personality was strong and resilient. The school was ethnically diverse, yet Ashley identified with the Jewish children. I then enrolled her in a preschool Sunday morning class at Briarwood Jewish Center.

For reasons I don't quite understand, when something is over I don't think about it again. I can't fathom how I could go from loving someone to not feeling anything about him at all. I felt like I did not care about Billy any longer. It was his life and I fought the best fight I could for us.

In truth, I never stopped worrying about him

122

Richmond Hill High School

Richmond Hill High School was a working class high school. Mainly, Italian, German, and Irish kids attended it. On my drug counseling caseload were kids who had come from families where drinking was the norm. Expectations for the future were low and there was little interest in investing time in their children's education.

Well, this would be easy. It was like being home again. The kids literally flocked to my office, although I was older than the typical new counselor. I was thirty-four years of age by this time. The majority of the faculty start when they are twenty-two, straight out of college. I was placed on the second floor in a very large space, due to the fact that I was required to run counseling groups. Word spread quickly that I was doing a great job with the kids. The only problem was that the kids were using me as their excuse to leave classes. The administration put a stop to this immediately, and rightfully so. The new rules were that if the students wanted to see me, it had to be during their lunch period.

The administration made me feel valued, and one particular person "in power" explained that if I went back to school in the summer and took twelve credits in education, I could be certified as a Guidance Counselor at a much higher pay rate. He stated that if I did that he would give me a job in September. That ignited another flame. So, there I was enrolling once again at Queens College for my education credits. This made a very large difference in not only my salary but in other things as well. It opened many life-enhancing options for me, making life quite a bit easier than before.

That September, there was a huge buyout for teachers. Most teachers are not happy human beings. No matter how one starts their career, with enthusiasm and vigor, it's hard to maintain the passion. When you begin your career, you don't see the obstacles you will have to endure. No one considers the push back from administrators or the consequences if they don't agree with your style of teaching. On so many levels, it imitates life as a student in high school. It's so important to be in the right "clique."

For me at that time, I was in the right "clique". Who doesn't love an enthusiastic, hard-working woman who has so much to prove and overcompensate for? I was not the brightest crayon in the box, however I did learn techniques on how to disguise my disabilities.

With the influx of new teachers and administrators, the Guidance position that was promised was no longer a shoo-in. The previous Assistant Principal had left and did not inform the new Principal of my qualities. It was required that I interview for the Guidance Counselor position.

There was plenty of gossip shared with me about the incoming administration. Who was competent and who was not. The new Principal was some hot shot from the Bronx, probably, in all honesty, just a good soldier. He was so inept. My inexperienced self knew he was not cut out for this job. There was quite a lot of hubbub about an incoming Assistant Principal of Guidance. His wife was just appointed Principal of August Martin High School. Most people did not say nice things about her personality. They also said that with her as Principal, their marriage was not going to make it through this school year. All of a sudden Richmond Hill was filled with psychics.

I received a letter from the new Acting Assistant Principal of Guidance with an appointment for an interview for the Guidance Counselor position. The word "acting" meant he was not actually given the position yet. Richmond Hill had the authority to give their feedback on his performance to the central office. Then he would go through a series of interviews before the position was authorized.

I was given a week's notice for this interview. Again, my panic attacks began. What if I don't get it? My brain has too many transmitters which send chemical messages to my body warning me that there is danger. Most of the time it is perceived danger, not actual. This is called Anxiety Disorder with Panic Attacks.

I had returned to an environment that instilled fear in me. Now I am working there and being interviewed to be one of them. This was way too much for me. I began regressing into my familiar sort of hell. It was just me and Ashley and I had to pretend and mask my anxiety to her when I came home. At school, it was happening all too often. The only way to survive was to befriend someone and share what I was experiencing, or I would lose my job. There was a position in each school hired by the UFT, for teacher support. It was a private office and everything was confidential. The person I talked to was Diana Mann. At the time, I felt like I was on a ledge of a building ready to jump. The feeling of a panic attack is the scariest feeling, the most horrendous experience I have ever had. That remains true to this day. For me, my anxiety was that they were going to find out that I was a fraud. I had no business being a professional counselor, and this man, Jay Gurka, Acting A.P., was going to know it during my interview process.

Diana helped talk me down from that ledge. I would vomit in the morning and in the evening. She roleplayed the interview with possible questions. Her devotion was the only reason I was not walking out on this interview.

The day of the interview she walked me downstairs to the office where the interview was being held, hugged me and said, *"You can do this."* Diana was standing there when I came out. Enough cannot be said about what she did for me.

However, Jay Gurka, Acting A.P., turned out to be a real prick in this interview. He bombarded me with questions as fast as bullets and didn't give me much time to think about my answers. That worked out actually well. I knew the answers. I didn't know I had any confidence in myself. There were only two candidates; me with zero experience and another woman with fifteen years under her belt.

That evening Mr. Gurka called my house and Ashley, at the age of four at the time, answered and called me to the phone. Mr. Gurka introduced himself and the very first thing he said was, *"Who was that?"* I was taken aback by the question. I thought to myself, *"What does this have to do with anything?"* He said *"I can't believe you have a daughter."* It sounded like there was disappointment in his voice. He told me I had gotten the job and was very impressed by the quickness and the ability to answer the questions so competently. He stated that I needed to go down to the Board of Education and change my status to a Board of Education employee. Prior to that, I was working for the drug program called SPARK, which was a state-run program. It took three months to process the paperwork. It was going to be a new opportunity after all!

It finally happened and I was sitting inside the Guidance Suite with all the other Guidance Counselors. What a trip. I made my office beautiful and welcoming, something I didn't see any of the other counselors doing. It was a metaphor for how they felt about their job. The dictionary defines a job as "a place of work, especially a specific task done as a routine of one's occupation." I guess that says it all.

It was anything but a job to me, however. It was an affirmation that I had a place of value in society. I mattered and I was going to make kids feel that they mattered, too. I loved my involvement with my students at Richmond Hill.

My way of doing things were not traditionally the way things were done. I touched and hugged students when they needed comfort. I did not worry about implications of any sort. My office and all Guidance offices were made of see through glass. Everything was visible at all times. People need human touch from birth or we don't thrive. The proper touch, the kind that is welcoming and loving, is so critical. We live in a basically non-touch society. People know immediately if a touch doesn't feel right. They recoil.

I created mother and daughter evening counseling at Richmond Hill High School. I felt very strongly about issues that would continually arise among our female students, and with their relationships with their mothers. These issues needed to be addressed.

I held my group on Tuesday evenings at 7 pm so that the mothers could come after work. I had eight sets of mothers and daughters. It took a few weeks for things to become a little comfortable. In groups, people usually take on the roles that they experience in real life. So for example, you have the leader, the drama queen, the victim, and always the ones who want to remain invisible.

I had taken interest in this one female I was counseling consistently, twice every week. She was very bright and hysterically funny. Like a female version of John Leguizamo. She was half Puerto Rican and half Dominican and was the oldest child in the family. Her mother was a domestic worker and her father was a chronic alcoholic. She would cry so hard at our sessions it sounded as if it was coming from deep down in her belly. It was heart breaking to listen to. She would have literal tantrums in class when she felt overwhelmed and distraught. I would hold her and talk her down. Her behavior scared school employees. They thought she was a threat to others. I vouched for her behavior and said that I could help her.

It was about that time when Billy moved out and perhaps caring for her filled a void in my life and kept the crazy in, but once removed. In hindsight, it was not professional to be so close to her. First, I gave her my telephone number. Gradually I invited her into my home. It felt empowering for me! I was saving a woman, wasn't I?

After a month of the Mother and Daughter group, her mother said that *"if I was doing so well with her, why don't I take care of her?"* And I did. I took her home with me. It filled me up like chicken soup on a cold day. I was used to taking care of people, and Ashley would have a "sister" to talk to. I made the rules and she followed them for a while. The one issue we always butted heads about was her pot smoking. We fought, she would leave, and then she would come back again. We loved each other like mother and daughter. Ash also loved her. She remained at Richmond Hill High School, although I did not.

Once I left Richmond Hill, this young woman became a larger part of our life. She attended holiday dinners and graduations and all things that families do. She attended Borough of Manhattan Community College. She graduated and her mother did not attend. I did! I was so proud of her achievements. In reality, I internalized them as my achievements also. I needed to believe I was valuable and had an impact on her life.

As time went on, life became filled with resentments and disagreements. The lines were very blurry. Who was receiving more joy from the relationship? I still don't have an answer. For her 30th birthday, we were going on our annual February vacation. I wanted to take her with us, she had never gone on vacation before (I had never traveled until I was 35 years old either) and I wanted to show her what it felt like. I wanted her to unlearn what she felt about herself. When we arrived in Puerto Vallarta, she and Ash shared a room. It was beautiful there. A day later, she became withdrawn and was exhibiting strange behavior. She became agitated and angry, did not want to sit with us or eat with us. I asked her what was wrong and she said she was depressed and wanted to be back in her own apartment.

I starting seeing her differently, almost like someone with a personality disorder. Upon arriving home things really became crazy. We took a taxi from Kennedy Airport. At this time, I knew she lived in Brooklyn, by the Verrazano Bridge. I asked her to please pay attention because I did not know how to tell the taxi driver to go. She, however, paid none because she was so agitated. The taxi driver was already in Queens when both she and I got in a horrendous fight. I screamed at her, *"Why aren't you paying attention?"* I said. *"This is costing me more money. You don't appreciate what I have done for you."* At that moment, she became so enraged that I don't think she was able to see things clearly. She screamed at me in Spanish for over ten minutes. The only thing I can remember her saying out loud and in English was, *"You are the neediest bitch I have ever met."* I was devastated. We drove to my house and she called her mother and asked for someone to pick her up.

She waited in the street, then left. I never saw her again.

In the years since this incident, I have gone over my role in this scenario many times and have tried to dissect this relationship and my motives with a couple of shrinks. It is clear that in my first year of being a Guidance Counselor, I was not aware of the boundaries in working with my students. Being newly single, I tried too hard to fill the void. I told myself that I was helping and saving a girl and that made me my own hero, in my own mind, anyway.

I will never in life forget the impact of our relationship. I know now it was not therapeutically ethical, however I loved her and valued our relationship. I think about her all the time and hope she has found the love that she so deserves.

Mr. Gurka

Richmond Hill was in transition, the student body was slowly changing as the neighborhood changed largely to accommodate Guyanese families. The older teachers with some years behind them hated the change and how it impacted the school.

There are many stages to change, and they are rarely simple. There is no easy way to transition. Everyone acts out differently, some people experience anger, discouragement, and others adjust and even feel hopeful and motivated. It all happens gradually. People like to get ready for the change to happen, like getting a new administration in their school where they have been working for years. Workers in general like to be prepared to see the change coming, however that's not what happened here.

Mr. Gurka was an enigma; he wore a suit and did what was expected of him. He would be the one to get it done, one that plays by the rules. No more, no less. His impression was that of a sad man. His hair looked unwashed and his gait was not peppy. He was traditional by all counts. He was also not the most motivated of men. In short, he didn't look like someone who yearned for recognition or power.

When Mr. Gurka came to Richmond Hill, I doubt he wanted to be the center of attention. Let's just say he was not going to win the Mr. Congeniality Contest. He was in charge of the admission process which meant he interviewed potentially new students. In the days, before "the Mr. Gurka Era," the system would filter out kids they deemed unsuccessful. They did not care about the kids directly, they cared about statistics and success. This was so that the school looked favorable and would attract good students who would want to attend this neighborhood school.

The faculty became very upset as the tenor of the school changed and blamed him for the cultural changes that were occurring. He was the victim of this change. This exclusion of certain types of students was systemic. All school administrators were guilty of foul play.

Mr. Gurka had started to feel the chill in the air and would find himself an outsider, except in my office. He was trying to make a friend out of a new player who was not committed to the old rules. It worked but not in way that everyone thought. At least, not for a while. He definitely was not particularly attractive to me because he was Caucasian!

I was happy to encourage him; I liked his values and tried hard to keep him motivated.

The school year was moving swiftly and it was time for me to make arrangements for one particular male student on my caseload to attend summer camp. He had lost both his parents to AIDS. It was the very early part of 1991 and AIDS was killing many people, including my friend Christine, the school Social Worker. I called up Big Brother to see if there was a camp that he could attend for a bit of an escape from his grief. I found a place where this student could go; however, he had no clothing for camping. My colleague suggested to me that I should ask Mr. Gurka for old clothes from his two sons. I got enough nerve to ask him, and he said, *"Of course!"*

The following day, Mr. Gurka turned into Jay! He brought in two very large bags of designer clothes. I way so happy, not only for my student, but that Jay could be so kind and generous. I started looking at him in a whole new light.

May was upon us and Jay was called into the Superintendent's Office for a review. I had not known this. Why should I have? It was the end of the day and Jay came into my office looking really upset. I just looked up and he grabbed my arm and asked me to follow him. Of course I did.

He knew the classrooms and their layouts much more than I did as I rarely left my 1st floor office. He took me to an art room, fairly private, with a large ledge and we sat down. He began to cry ever so softly to relay the events of what had just occurred. He explained that they were not even allowing him to go through the interview process for the official title of Assistant Principal. This was so hurtful to him on so many levels. His wife was officially the Principal of a high school in Queens and now he was not even going to get the A.P. job that he had worked so hard for. It seems that influential members of the faculty felt that

Jay was so well connected that he would automatically get the job, and they wanted to avoid that possibility.

I remained quiet. What could I say? The room was silent and we were sitting side by side. He touched my hand for the first time and said, *"I have been married to one woman my whole life."* I was so nervous. Truth be told, I was in a relationship, then a marriage with the same man for fourteen years. Both of us had very little experience outside of our one relationship. Both us were with our mates since we were twenty years of age. I was then thirty–five and he was forty-five years old.

Wearing the letter "A"

In June, we attended our school's prom. His wife and her school was one floor beneath ours. This catering hall was a popular venue for proms. Leslie, Jay's wife, decided to come up and meet the Guidance Counselor that was so fabulous at her job. Maybe it was women's intuition. She introduced herself and said, *"I wanted to meet the counselor Jay always talks about. Maybe I'll steal you for my school."*

That night it was clear to both of us that we were attracted to one another. We began to meet at parks and just talk for hours. One day he asked if he could meet Ashley who was five years old at the time. He suggested that we go to IHOP. Which kid does not love pancakes? Little did he know that it was my favorite breakfast food, too. Ash was more comfortable than expected. She said, *"This feels like a family."*

When I was married to Billy we never ever went out for breakfast. That was a real luxury. Going to dinner once in a while was a treat, but to pay for eggs or pancakes when

I could easily make them for pennies did not make economic sense when you don't have money.

Camp Chipinaw

It was the end of June and Jay and I were not returning to Richmond Hill High School in the fall. He did not get the job and my position was cut with the budget cuts that following school year. Jay and I still had not consummated our relationship. I would not sleep with him knowing he was leaving on July 1st for his summer job that he and his wife had held for seventeen years. It was at a sleep away camp, up in the Catskill Mountains. He loved camp, he loved being with the same familiar faces each summer. Working also allowed his sons to attend camp for free.

Everyone knew what they were doing each summer. Both Jay and Leslie loved structure and continuity, at any cost. It was also a way to save all summer on food and bills for their home in Queens and save all the money they made at camp for their sons' college education. Jay's job was a Tennis Director. Leslie was head of girls' side at the camp. She always held the higher position. Leslie was hungry for power and everyone knew it. She was Principal during the school year and still in power during the summer as head of the female staff at summer camp.

July 22

My birthday is July 22.

In camp, you are committed for the first week without a day off. There were no cell phones then, but there were pay phones in town. The only phone in camp was in the main office. It took a lot of motivation and endurance for Jay to want to call me. He did. Every day I stayed home waiting for him to call me. It could not be long calls because you needed so much change, it felt like every second the operator would say your three minutes are up. It was not a good feeling at all knowing Jay was married. In fact, it made me feel quite ill.

After the first week, they had every Wednesday off. On the third day off, Jay called me and asked if he could see me for my birthday. It just so happened that day fell on a Wednesday. Leslie would go to see her mother and normally Jay would go home and take care of the bills and laundry.

Jay had one friend that he could confide in at camp. His name was Bruce. Bruce volunteered his apartment so Jay could bring me there for our first interlude.

Both of us were scared out of our minds, not knowing what to do first. I will never forget the first time he looked at me without clothing. It was like he was looking at the most beautiful woman in the world, his eyes said it all.

Fall of 1992

Jay moved in with me with the commitment of marriage. I would not have let any man move in with Ashley and me without this commitment. Jay was definitely not the type of man to make a promise and not follow through. However, it lingered in my mind like an endless night. It just sat in my belly all wrong. It had been so awful for me to accept that I was somehow involved in the dissolution of his marriage. I felt that he did not handle the breakup in an honorable way.

Jay is definitely non-confrontational. He tends to avoid conflict at all costs. In all honesty, it was probably one of the issues in their marriage. Jay was not a go-getter kind of man. However, this was not an excuse. He had a responsibility to communicate to Leslie about his unhappiness. I did have a problem with this sort of dishonesty. I went over the "rules" of our relationship. The number one nonnegotiable issue was that he must be communicative and honest. I did not ever want to be blindsided by his dishonesty.

There were parts of Jay that were like an enigma. He could seem detached yet break a tennis racket if he didn't like the way he was playing. I would question him for quite a while about not loving Leslie. Why did he not leave before? Didn't the boys notice that your marriage was not one of a loving nature? He could not answer me.

A Brief Overview

Jay's parents were survivors of the Holocaust in

Holland, where Jay was born. They endured the horrors

that we read about but really could not imagine such as

drinking your own urine because you were so dehydrated.

His mother had to self-abort a pregnancy during wartime

because she refused to bring a child into this sort of hell.

His mother and father were hidden in eleven different

homes by brave and generous Gentile people who housed

them purely out of a sense of doing the right thing. In their

last home, they stayed with their families in the attic, but

were permitted to go downstairs at night to get some food.

One night, Jay's mother and father were downstairs when

the deafening noise of Gestapo broke down the front door.

It was that evening that his parents had to run out the back

door in their pajamas. Everyone upstairs was captured and

taken to concentration camp. His parents roamed the streets

until they were caught and imprisoned until the end of the

war. They came here by boat and landed on Ellis Island in

1952. They spent a week on Ellis Island until they were finally permitted to enter the country.

In typical fashion, Jay told me about having fun with his younger brother on the boat that brought them over. Children were allowed to run around freely and play while most adults were vomiting, sickened by the turbulence of the waters. Families with the least amount of money were confined to rooms below deck.

Maybe that is Jay's built-in defense mechanism, to block out the bad and survive on the good. He was a very bright student who attended Stuyvesant High School; at the time it was all boys! He attended school with many accomplished students. Jay again gave his bare minimum. It is his personality and objective to be invisible.

His dad had been a very nervous man, unable to drive. But he loved to sing. His mom was the one who would make frequent trips to the airport to bring people home. She worked full time and never complained about her loveless marriage.

Back to Chipinaw

Jay returned to camp and the second week of August he told each of his sons separately that he was moving out. He then proceeded to tell Leslie. A turbulent year followed for Leslie and she is not the type of woman who takes things sitting down. Nor should she, in my opinion.

Leslie being Principal in a Queens High School and me being a lowly Guidance Counselor in Queens did not make for a comfortable situation for all concerned. She called into "the old boys club" and word was out! Randi Gurka stole my husband and no one is to treat her kindly. Everyone was afraid of her wrath and so they complied with her demands.

September rolled around and I was placed at Flushing High School under the supervision of one of the oldest Principals in Queens. I am not referring to his age; I am talking about his years of service. That counted big time back then. I was in deep shit. Everything I did was observed. My Assistant Principal, who was my direct supervisor, was harshly overcompensating his loyalty to Leslie. All the other women counselors were cold and not helpful at all. I was the youngest counselor with the least experience. They viewed me as a woman who could not be trusted.

Every month there was a Principal's meeting held at a different school. When the meeting was at Flushing High, I was directed not to leave my room and was not even allowed to walk the building.

If that shit was to happen now, you can believe I would not be that sweet naive woman who smiled and was nice to everyone. I hated that school, it was filled with people who were narrow minded and righteous assholes who thought they were smarter and better and reveled in being in the "Lets Hate Randi Club."

I would go home every day to Jay and tell him that I don't think this relationship is worth this sort of angst. Then he would spend the evening convincing me that it is

151

all worth it because he loved me and was going to make my life better than I could have ever imagined.

I would then get up and face another day, and with each passing day I would tell myself that this is not the be-all and end-all. Three years later, the divorces were final. Jay and I got married. I invited one person from that school. I was quite amused when the other counselors wanted to know why they were not invited.

(Regretfully, Leslie Gurka passed away prematurely after I had completed the final draft of this book.)

My Father

After many years of not being in touch with my father, I reached out to him to tell him that I was getting married. In fact, my husband to be was Jewish. This is important, because when I married Billy and my father disowned me, he told me that if I ever get divorced, a white man would never touch me ever again. He viewed me as a leper.

It has been my life experience that the hardest thing for me to accept is that people rarely, if ever change. I still allowed my father to hurt me. When was I going to stop him from doing this? I could not stop him, but I could stop myself from caring, and that's what I did.

A Continuation Therapy

I made many attempts to find a good therapist. I tried some for a few visits and then felt that they just did not get me. My anger was choking me to death and at times, I felt it oozing out of my body. Work at school sucked, money was being stretched and the stressors that Jay's sons were became nearly intolerable. To top it off, Jay did not come home till almost seven on most weekdays because he was officiating soccer, basketball and softball games to bring in more money. Honestly, I think that was only half the reason. Jay got to be the important man everyday with his black whistle around his neck, making the calls: "You are out!" No one could question his authority and it was always his call. Even I couldn't compete with that power. It was his time to shine in his quirky uniform, like an overgrown kid. My search continued for just one therapist to guide me down this fucking path alive.

Ashley

I constantly worried about Ash also. Would she adjust to living with Jay? We bought a rundown condo townhouse in a very Jewish area in Bayside. I did not want to live there. I was totally out of my comfort zone. Living white and Jewish was not something that came naturally to me.

Jay once again promised me that, although this was not my dream house, it was what we could afford given that both of his sons were in college at the same time. The boys are seventeen months apart in age.

Moving into that development was like moving into a kibbutz ("a collective community in Israel"). People looked out their windows when you got home, monitoring your routine, asking questions. It felt like living in a fish bowl.

Ashley had a hard time as well. Someone asked if she was adopted. I explained to Ash that her response to those nosy people should be this: *"I came from mommy's belly and my father is black."* I was convinced that we didn't fit in there.

Billy never saw Ash anymore, so the people in the neighborhood never saw him either.

As far as school went, she was always intellectually gifted and most kids gravitated to her. In fourth grade, Ashley got the lead in the school play, "The Wiz." We had no idea that she had the confidence to take on the lead. It took a lot of courage. But with that courage she became very popular and self-assured.

In the sixth grade Ashley's doctor recommended we take her for an orthopedic consult. He thought her spine was not growing straight. We took her to a recommended specialist in the Bronx who confirmed the diagnosis as curvature of the spine. It is called Scoliosis. This was devastating for my beautiful twelve-year-old baby. She was forced to wear a full brace from her waist to her neck. It was to be worn twenty–three hours a day. Every three weeks we had to take her to a technician who made adjustments while Ashley continued to grow. This was a defining time in her life. The heat of the summer was almost unbearable for her. Kids were always asking her

156

what was wrong. It took a lot of cajoling to keep her in that brace. Four years of wearing this brace prevented her from having a steel rod placed in her back. She wore the brace until ninth grade when she refused to wear it anymore.

Jay's Sons

Jay's sons had great loyalty to their mom; this is

not uncommon for sons of the jilted spouse. They were young men, aged 19 and 18 years. For the first two years I agreed to be held hostage to their demands. I was not allowed to pick up my home phone (still no cell phones existed) in case they called. The boys did not want to meet me. They resisted seeing their father. This was so painful for Jay. This made him unconsciously withdraw from Ashley in those first couple of years.

I didn't understand how he couldn't love this little adorable five year old. Jay's guilt was cumbersome, a heavy weight he could not discard. Nothing worked. I am sure I had a lot to do with this. I overcompensated and tried very hard be to be liked by Jay's sons. The harder I tried the more vulnerable I made myself. It took many years of being disrespected and objectified that Jay and I decided to seek out a skilled therapist to resolve our extended family issues.

The impetus was that Jay and I had been invited to his younger son's and wife's home to view their wedding album. His younger son was a conflicted young man. He and I cared about each other a lot, however his guilt for these feelings always came with a set of retaliations. He had cooked all day so that I would be proud of his culinary skills. We shared our love of good food and took great pride in feeding others. Right before dinner, the wedding album was brought out for viewing. It was handed to me first. I perused the album, and with each passing page I felt bile entering my throat. I did not know if I could keep down the vomit. Nowhere in that album was there a single picture of me. Ashley was one of the bridesmaids and she was intentionally also left out. This was one of those no turn back moments for me. I could not swallow back what I was choking on. I turned to Jay and asked to leave. His son bounded out of his chair so violently I honestly thought he was going to hit me. He didn't but we left anyway. This incident was a game-changer.

With gentle, thoughtful words coming from our therapist, we worked on why Jay could not let go of his fantasy of us being one happy family. It was so heartbreaking watching his tears run down his cheeks. He choked on his words. Jay had endured too many years of rejection from his sons.

Jay is not a dreamer. That is my role in the family. He is steadfast and very literal. In this case, he owned it and realized that he had lost his sons when he left their mother for me.

That is how it remains, no seeing each other for birthdays, no holiday dinners, only obligatory phone contact. Jay's anxiety level reaches a point where his legs tremble when they are talking. How can a father be discarded because he no longer loved their mother? He still loved them!

Jay was the one to lie up all night when they were sick or injured. He protected them when they got into trouble. Jay even protected them from their mom. Why could they not see what was right in front of them?

Life as Three!

Ashley was about seven years old when Jay stepped into the deep end of the pool. He actively accepted the role of her father. His first experience raising a female child was very intimidating. The second year together Jay wanted to take us skiing. Ash and I had never been. We were not that enthusiastic about being cold and sleeping in a cabin. The first morning we went skiing, it was confirmed that we both didn't like bundling up, especially with those boots that weigh a ton. Before we even reached the ski slope, Ashley fell. Jay and I told her to stop whining because she was cold and had only fallen in place. Ash continued to cry about her leg hurting. I told Jay that it was not like her to continue to complain without a reason. It turned out that Ashley's leg was broken!

For the next six weeks Jay carried Ashley to her classroom and placed her in a foldable lounge chair at the front of her classroom every morning. Lunch would be brought to her every day and different friends would keep her company. He had quickly learned we weren't cut out to be skiers.

Ashley won the National History Award and traveled to the state level competition in Cooperstown, N.Y. They both went without me. Ashley's best friend at the time went with her dad. The dads slept in the same room and the girls had their own room. Ashley now had exactly what I had always wanted her to have: a real father. He always participated in everything; Open School Night, doctor's appointments, dances and continual help in math. I could not help there.

At the beginning of our cohabitation, we all needed a transitional time to adjust to the new life. I had slept in the same bed with Ash since she was born. It was clear that that arrangement had to change. Ashley did not like this one little bit, her revenge was that I needed to sit on the sofa in her sight until she fell asleep. This idea was absurd to Jay. His parenting skills are the very opposite of mine. After all, he raised boys. I spent months reassuring Ashley that I was not going to vanish while at the same time I had to deal with Jay's sulking because he did not receive much attention from me. Maybe this was our first real power struggle. Who was more important? I was not going to play this game with him. Ash is my daughter and she came out of my body. She, to me, would always come first.

With time, we reached our comfort zones and our new roles were established. Our family was finding a steady flow.

Money was very restrictive for about five years. The lawyers were paid off. Jay and Leslie reached a financial agreement. There, however, was one issue that still needed to be resolved. Leslie was observant of Jewish laws. One of the rules was that if you want a divorce, the husband had to grant it to his wife. It is called a "get." "The essential part of the "get" is very short; the text states "you are hereby permitted to all men," which means the woman is no longer married and adultery no longer applies. A certificate is handed to the husband and ripped into small pieces then handed back to the wife representing the dissolution of the union.

The divorce would not have happened if Jay did not grant the "get." Leslie would not be able to marry a Jewish man unless she had a paper to prove she is now divorced under Jewish law.

This is a brutal and antiquated law for me. The thought of erasing years or eliminating a union is absurd. I was never into organized religion, or the laws to dictate what is right or wrong. Watching Jay come home from this "ceremony", of sorts, was so wrenching to see. He walked in as if he had just lost half of himself. He probably had, truth be told.

Marriage

$\mathbf{G}$etting married for me felt like validation that I was worth being part of another person's life. Honestly, it took so many years of dissecting and reframing all horrible statements that had broken me into pieces. As sad as it was, it was going to take patience and love which only a man like Jay could give. Try to imagine taking a five hundred-piece puzzle and pissing all over it and then asking someone to put the puzzle together. Then once it's placed together, put it on display for all to see. The net worth is unimaginable!

I needed so badly to become a woman who felt worthy of devotion, love, gentleness, and consistency. To have all three of us treated with worthiness, even at moments when our most admirable traits did not shine, and to continue to be loved boggles my mind. It is rare when a union is unconditional and not hurtful. Until I met Jay, I had never thought this union could exist. "Daddy issues" may be alive and well, but not for long.

We had a small wedding in our small new home. It felt large and grand enough for the entire world to see. Hors d'oeuvres were doled out, made from the freshest of ingredients. A violinist and a cellist played as I walked down the staircase that I had wrapped in lace. I was so happy that day. Ashley sang "Home" from Beauty and the Beast and had everyone in tears, including the servers. I did not allow my thoughts of his son's disapproval taint my wedding day. I am positive that they would have rather had root canal than attend their father's wedding.

The divorce was finalized in early February and we were married in March. I hated Monday mornings like everyone else, but this Monday was different. I was now Mrs. Jacob Gurka! All those people who bet against us lost their money.

Soon after, I asked to be released from Flushing High School and to be transferred to somewhere where I would be treated fairly.

Springfield Gardens High School

This was my first experience with a female Principal and her female Assistant Principal of Guidance. And what a pleasure it was! In this interview, I explained the injustices that I experienced from the previous male Principals. This Principal knew Leslie Gurka and had heard the rumblings of gossip. She made it very clear to me that I would be judged only by my intuition and competence on the job, nothing else. I was loved and truly felt supported by all the women colleagues at my school. I was slowly beginning to navigate the waters of being a Guidance Counselor. My students loved me and the administration valued me. I became a confident professional. I felt like the "A" was either fading or possibly disappearing from my world.

After four years at Springfield Gardens High School, my respected Principal retired due to an illness, later to find out it was breast cancer.

As a result, there was a new administration. They brought in a physical education teacher who was not up to the task of Principal. He was placed there because he was a good soldier, and he was promised this position if he waited patiently. He did. The school had become a low functioning school at this juncture. What harm could he do? Plenty was the answer. The violence escalated, academic expectations lowered and the school became a place of racial divide. The largest ethnic population was families of West Indian descent. Parents would come in with their children's poor report cards and wanted to know what I was going to do to salvage their child. Trickle down effects were becoming apparent: students no longer excelled, teachers began watering down the academic expectations, and a passive principal who was African-American was not taking a stand to provide a positive learning environment. Bottom line was that when people don't feel valued and respected it becomes a hostile place to be in.

The Big "C"

I was forty-three at this time; my sister Lori, married with two daughters and residing in Colleyville, Texas got the horrific news that she had very aggressive breast cancer. I was devastated when I heard that. As her big sister, I needed to care for her. I took a family emergency week off to spend time with my sister in Texas.

I have a knack of being funny in times of crisis. I made a sign saying Lori's Baptist Church, so that when people walked into her bedroom the black mood would be broken, even for a couple of moments. I started to dance as though I was in a church choir and everyone was praying for Lori! She began to laugh. There goes my crazy sister Randi with her silly pranks. Anything for a laugh, I thought.

After a couple of days of emptying her drains and nights filled with sisters crying, it became clear how serious this was. Lori's chest wall was turning black from dying tissue, known as necrosis. It was heartbreaking going through this with my mother and now with my baby sister. My heart was breaking.

After a week I had to return to work. Each day at lunchtime I would go to my car and cry. I felt so helpless not being there with her. What if she dies? The doctor explained that this sort of cancer was so much more aggressive than my mom's. They can actually compare the different genes and their mutations. They could not do reconstructive surgery; Lori did not have any healthy skin left to build pockets for the implants. It takes over a year to grow healthy tissue to place expanders in, to stretch out the skin. This process is very painful.

Her oncologist suggested to Lori that her two sisters get tested for the BRCA 1 and 2-gene mutation. It is most common in Jewish women of Ashkenazi descent. Since two main family members had already suffered from the disease, we now had to see what our chances were.

I made an appointment with a Hereditary Geneticist. I had to take a blood test and sign papers that stated that they could not violate the act of privacy, no matter what the results were. It took six weeks for the results to come back, and I had to be physically present to get the results.

As the weeks progressed, I told myself over and over again that this could not happen to me. I was a good person. I took care of my crazy father and in light of all my suffering I should be exempt from this fate.

Jay and I drove to the hospital and took the elevator to the sixth floor. A very slow elevator made its way up as my anxiety level rose higher. I tried to pray away the results. As we opened the door of the Social Worker's office, her expression was all I needed to see to know the results. I collapsed into my husband's arms and wept. This wasn't fair. Gasping for air and snot running down my face, I was yelling and crying *"No!"* This can't be happening to me.

After some water and a discussion of what was to be done next, I was in a total fog. Within two weeks of finding out my results, I scheduled myself for a total hysterectomy. Estrogen feeds breast cancer cells. Therefore it is essential to remove the estrogen in order to decrease the likelihood of getting cancer. I was told that without the surgery, I would be at an extremely high risk of developing cervical or ovarian cancer before I was seventy years old.

No One Tells The Truth

I had my list of questions for the surgeon. None of them were answered truthfully! I asked if I would get hot flashes, he said no. How bad is the pain? He responded, *"You will feel some discomfort."* I had the surgery in a hospital in the Bronx. When I woke up after six hours of surgery, I felt like I was hit by a doublewide. I was looking up at a nurse who whispered, *"Your body has been through an extensive trauma."* I had lost a lot of blood and had received multiple blood transfusions. No one had presented me with the possible scenarios of what might happen with such an extensive surgery.

I was in a suite of six women. The constant smell of urine assaulted my senses. The hospital was filled with foreign noises. Big, cranky nurses walked around not responding to anyone's needs. I asked to please be taken to the bathroom, as the drain that had been inserted would extend from my bladder to the bag of urine, which was filled to the brim. Eventually I stretched my weak legs to the edge of the bed and urinated on the floor. It was utterly disgusting there.

My stay in the hospital would last three full days, with Jay always by my side. Ashley was afraid to come to the hospital to see me. Jay reassured her that I was going to be fine in a few weeks. If she came to the hospital, he would stay by her side at all times. She did not have to be afraid. As Ash walked into the suite, a ray of sunshine followed her like a rainbow follows a storm. Jay knew how I felt about Ash. If she could not bring me joy, no one could. So he brought me my bundle of joy!

They removed my uterus, my ovaries, my cervix, and my fallopian tubes. The weeks that followed, I felt like I was a flat noodle, unable to lift myself out of bed for bodily functions. I could not even lift the blanket when I felt warm. Jay once again demonstrated his dedication to me; he had to carry me around with my arms wrapped around his head to prevent me from falling. I believe it was then that I truly believed that he loved me, and that I found a home in his arms.

There is one huge deficit in Jay's personality; he is allergic to the kitchen. I lost a great deal of weight not being able to cook as a result of my low energy levels. My diet consisted of takeout pizza and Chinese food served in the box on the bed.

In the following months, my hormones depleted what was left in my body and I nosedived into all sorts of symptoms. I had the worst case of hot flashes that left me so humiliated at work. I would perspire so intensely that the papers on my desk needed to be moved so that they would not get caught in the down flow. Students would say to me, *"What's wrong, Miss?"* I had no answer for them or myself. The bouts of insomnia made me feel like I was on speed, my thoughts never stopped racing. I became agitated and impatient. I needed to see a psychiatrist to help me function. He placed me on Prozac, and Ambien for sleeping, which eased my symptoms, except for the hot flashes. They continued to plague me for the next fifteen years.

All Aboard for the Next Stop

Queens Vocational High School was my next school, and I thought my last. The Principal had already known about my abilities and my reputation. He was a very hard core Principal. If you did the right things he had your back, screw him and you are out. He was the youngest Principal to be appointed to that job, when he was in his early thirties. He remained in that school until his retirement, thirty odd years later.

I always functioned at my highest level when the playing field was equal. He was fair, consistent and rigid. He also had a side to him that was chivalrous. I would receive notes sporadically acknowledging my successes on the job.

One day I was in a meeting with the Principal reviewing students' progress when he shared with me that

175

his own father would smack him in the face when he did something wrong. I was taken aback that this man who can be cutting, sarcastic and harsh trusted me enough to share that intimate memory. I carry that moment with me always.

I prided myself on being transparent at all times.. The bathroom conversations were no longer about me. They were about others. Students, teachers and people in general would come into my office and share their most intimate feelings. I was called "Take it to the Grave Gurka." I never betrayed anyone's confidences.

This did not always play itself out, as it should have; there was a very intimidating and intoxicated Assistant Principal of Guidance. He would discuss details of his failing marriage and his children's failures in school. I knew it was not a good idea to be my supervisor's confidant. I also knew this was not going to end well. Things remained status quo as long as "my Principal" was there. However there was chatter that he was going to retire. He was planning to appoint a friend of my supervisor who was Assistant Principal of another department in this same school to the position of Interim Acting Principal.

My AP was afraid of the current Principal; he was aware that he did not like him and gave him a hard time. I became nervous that once my Principal retired, I would not have built in protection.

And so it happened. After years of loving my school and feeling comfortable with mostly all of the staff, "my Principal" retired. That following September, we started out with our new Principal (his buddy). The drinking became worse; everyone could smell the stale alcohol from the night before. People were talking and of course he did nothing about the rumors. If he took action, I was not aware of it. He became really grouchy and started making me defensive. He needed to show the new Principal that he was not weak and that he could write people up for their mistakes. He had never written anyone up in all the years I was working there, until now.

I never encouraged him in any way to have him think for one moment that I was attracted to him or anyone else. I was a happily married woman. Yet his covert attentions were always obvious to me.

It was Thanksgiving and many sad situations arose with the students. I got to know my students well. There was one particular pair of brothers that were living in a shelter in the Bronx. Their names were Kwan and Kadeem. They were living the American nightmare. Their mother was beaten down by men and society, and now they were homeless. For young black babies never to experience a man in their lives is an atrocity. They are left feeling contempt for all black men and resentment for the women who were left caring for them. Mirrors of their own images filled them with hurt and despair. It breaks their spirit and the ability to love and care for others.

I told the boys I would get them an already cooked turkey for their Thanksgiving dinner. Residents of shelters are not permitted to use hot plates of any sort due to the fire risk. On the Wednesday prior to Thanksgiving, I told their mother to come in and pick up the turkey. The whole family came in to retrieve their turkey and to say a big thank you to me. While we were enjoying the exchange of pleasantries, my office phone rang and it was a caseworker from an agency asking me to print out the attendance for another student. I indicated that this was not a good time because I was with a family.

When we returned from Thanksgiving break, I was asked into the Principal's office and was handed a "Write Up." Guess who found courage over that "lost weekend"? That same caseworker had called back and spoke to my A.P. that Wednesday and said that I had refused to give her the attendance. I explained to the Principal what had occurred, and standing by, as a witness, was the ball-less sad sack of an Assistant Principal. I was told that it did not matter if a family was getting a free turkey bought by me. This was my choice. The family could have waited. I fought back bringing in my UFT rep.

By now, it was becoming a power struggle between him and me. I would not pay attention to him and this was his retaliation. The atmosphere was again becoming tense. In June at the end of term party, this A.P. became so intoxicated, he tried to kiss me at the Guidance table and said, *"You know how badly I want you."*

I returned in September dreading work. I hated working for the Board of Education. Life took its ironic turn and I landed back into the school system that I had hated all along. I was trained to be a Family and Marriage Counselor, not to be someone's bitch in each school I worked in. I would go a couple of years not being harassed by one person or another, but eventually some insecure asshole would become my supervisor.

It was never about the kids. I loved them and they knew it. Somehow, I kept a bit of my belligerent self and would buck supervisors out of defiance. No matter how long I worked in the system, deep down I would never kowtow to "the man." It was always a male who challenged me; I always preformed my best with women. I love women. I look at how beautiful women are, how great they smell, and I am especially attracted to a woman who does her job well and does not get intimidated easily.

I have always been scared of men who are deep down weak but play oh so dirty. For the most part, I don't even like them. If my sexuality were not programmed to be heterosexual, I would hands down be with a woman.

Most of my experiences with women have been one of kinship. They are soft and willing to open their arms to hold you and comfort you. Not because they will harm you, but out of their purely natural way of nurturing one another.

Women Friends

It has always been difficult for me to make friends.

When I was young we could not and dared not bring anyone home to that crazy house. After that I had gotten all too soon into a relationship with a man who ensured that making friends remained only a fantasy. For most of my life, then, I had lived hiding under one rock or another. What a loss for me! I have craved real female friendships for as long as I can remember. I had gotten close to female friends twice but life either got in the way, or maybe I got in the way of things.

Wing Extension

I had another five years before I could retire.

Ashley was doing great in all aspects of life. Ashley is such a strong, independent young woman, the way I wish I could have been. We succeeded as parents, Jay and I. We could not have been more proud of her.

It was extremely difficult for me to allow my biracial daughter to attend, with academic scholarship, one of the whitest universities in the country, the University of Wisconsin in Madison. I started having concerns of how she would be treated, who were going to be her friends. Will she be safe? When Ash started UW, less than ten percent of the students were of color.

Ashley chose a Jewish dormitory for her freshman year. It was her chosen culture and where she felt she belonged. Needless to say, Ashley fit in beautifully in her new environment in her new school.

Ashley received a letter from the dorm stating who her roommate was going to be. The two of them wrote to each other for months trying to get a hold of what it would be like to live with one another. They discussed their likes and dislikes, and what their parents were responsible for, as far as dorm furniture was concerned.

It was very ironic that Anne, Ashley's new roommate, was slow on the processing procedure to secure a dorm that was right for her. Well, Anne was too late for the dorm of choice and landed up in "The Jewish Dorm."

A bit about Anne. Anne was from a small, all-white suburb of Chicago. Her father was an international attorney and was quite established. Anne has two sisters, both of whom were grooming themselves to work in the corporate world. Anne had never met a person of color or a Jewish person. I know this is quite hard to believe. However, this was true. Anne was now thick in the world of Jewish girls, an interesting situation for her, to say the least. Anne not only adjusted in her new environment, she blossomed in it. Ashley and Anne became the best of friends. Ash taught her all about her culture and Ashley learned more about "the real world" from Anne. At Easter, Anne's family invited Ashley to the country club for Easter egg hunt. It is where Ashley started to realize *"This isn't Kansas anymore.*" The people in attendance stared at her way harder than anywhere Ash had ever been.

Anne became involved with a Jewish boy; this was not what Anne's parents had anticipated for their daughter. The family of the Jewish boy was not too happy either. It had to end and it did.

It must be stated that Anne's parents are amazing people with generous souls and continue to still be part of Ashley's life.

Ash was so independent that she decided in her junior year of undergraduate school to spend a semester abroad. *"Great. Where do you want to go?" "University of Cape Town in South Africa."*

I didn't want her to be that independent. However, I never stifled her adventurous spirit. Just because I didn't have the wherewithal to even think about such an adventure doesn't mean that she couldn't think big either.

As with all students that go abroad, they need a complete physical examination. I went with Ashley to her doctor when she came home on a break. Two days later, at 10:30 in the evening, the doctor called our home and said that her blood test came out very abnormal and she needed

184

to come back the following day. We entered the exam room and were bludgeoned with a barrage of medical information. The only thing I heard was that was she needed to see a rheumatologist as soon as possible. There were weeks of different sorts of testing that left us with a sick feeling of dread. The doctor surmised that it was an autoimmune disease. We were given papers with descriptions of the symptoms and the various types of autoimmune diseases. However, they could not tell me what specific type she had. The disease had to play itself out. The doctor was very clear to Ash that she should pass on going to South Africa as her blood numbers were really bad.

Ash, being a determined young woman, responded through her tears, *"I am going."* She was not going to let this diagnosis interfere with her plans. I asked the doctor what steps I needed to take to make sure she remained healthy in South Africa, and other things I would need to do.

I had learned a long time ago that being resourceful was one of my greatest strengths. I started making calls to friends who connected me with the head of the Department of Rheumatology at the hospital in the University of Cape Town. I called him up. This doctor was very humble and explained to me that he was not only a doctor, but also a father. He would personally take her on for the five months she would be there. He gave me his personal telephone number. I still felt sick, however.

Jay and I took her to the airport for her life changing experience. How it was going to change our lives remained to be seen.

The first week, Ashley could not get her cell phone hooked up. We had to wait for two whole days to hear from her. When we finally did, it was not pleasant. She was in a tiny room by herself outside of a larger house where four other students from all different countries resided. All the windows had bars. She was not allowed to go out unless accompanied by another student. I never underestimated her guts, but this was totally out my comfort zone. I don't think Ash anticipated just how different a third world country would be.

The students would not begin classes for another week. Ashley was crying on the phone and I begged her to come home almost every day that she was there. A young man, like many college students, drank to excess and vomited all over her front door. How was she going to clean this up? I surely could not help her with this one.

After two weeks of classes Ashley had a flare up! A flare up is when your immune system attacks normal cells. She became ill and called the doctor at Cape Town Hospital. As promised, he placed her on a steroid medication to reduce the swelling in her legs. He did reach out to us by phone and promised me that this regimen was going to reduce her symptoms and she would get better. I, however, did not entirely trust him.

I probably cut off a couple of years from Jay's life; he now had to worry about both of us.

We planned a trip to South Africa for Ashley's spring break. We could have flown without a plane if there was a way to do that – that is how much we missed her. We scheduled a two-week trip to Africa, one week in Cape Town and the second in Zimbabwe and Botswana for a safari.

Our flight was at 10 pm and I was tired and scared. It was to be a 20-hour trip. I knew that if Ashley could do this alone, then I could do it too. I had the safety of being with my husband that Ashley didn't have when she had travelled. Let me digress here for a little while. Before I met Jay, I had never left New York City. People who grow up in poverty are the most afraid of exploring the uncertain. If you live in an insecure environment and your home isn't the safe place that it is supposed to be, then everything else, by extension, also becomes unsafe and very scary.

All of my students who had grown up like me never even entertained going away to college. People who have grown up around dysfunctional people use their senses much more than the average Joe. For example, my sense of smell and the memories that linger are extremely potent. Once your olfactory sense is assaulted, your brain is hard wired to remember sights and smells. I can always retrieve the smell of my father's oily hair, or the smell of my grandmother in a nursing home, gumming a half of a peanut butter sandwich. These are scents that never leave you.

I can still smell my mother-in-law's sweet breath. My husband's breath is the same. Maybe it's the natural smell of sweetness that is pervasive in their souls.

188

Those smells are as beautiful as spring when you don't live in Flushing, Queens.

When we boarded the plane we removed our shoes for the twenty-hour pilgrimage. Everything was fine until we stopped in Senegal to refuel. It was then that the smells of a foreign land arrived. The smell of people who had traveled for a great many hours and had not washed was penetrating my nose. I had to remind myself to be grateful for such an extravagant trip. This sort of journey was meant for the elite. Am I that sort of person now? The kind of person I had always hated?

Brushing my teeth has always been a metaphor for overall good hygiene for me. When traveling for long periods of time, sleeping off and on, your mouth becomes so yucky. I needed to brush my teeth immediately! I entered the plane's bathroom and was so disoriented that I dropped my toothbrush in the toilet. Teeth-brushing is one of my obsessions. How was I going to stay in this plane with bad breath? My father always reminded me when my breath wasn't minty fresh. The possible loss of my toothbrush left me feeling humiliated. What was I to do? I have always been resourceful. I asked the flight attendant for boiling water so that I could sterilize my toothbrush. The thought of that experience still makes me feel like throwing up. But you do what you need to do. The rest of our flight was uneventful.

Ashley met us at our hotel in town. We held each other and cried, so happy to be in each other's arms. It had been two excruciatingly long months.

Our hotel in Cape Town was beautiful with a wonderful shower. We all couldn't wait to jump in. Ashley's normal accommodations were frugal and bare at best. Our shower looked like something out of a magazine to all of us. We chose who got to go first, and of course, Ashley won.

The following day, we visited the prison at Robben Island, where Mandela spent eighteen out of his twenty-seven year sentence. An actual former political prisoner showed us around. We learned so much. I loved to learn about history but Ash, not so much.

The food was so foreign to me. That's where I was outnumbered. Jay and Ashley were open to trying anything. I was more willing to starve than I was to eat Kudu or Warthog.

Off we went to meet a pilot who was taking us in a passenger plane for four. We left from Cape Town to Kruger National Park. I sat next to the pilot on a trip I will never forget. The wheels of the plane lifted us off the ground and we flew so gently over the greenest bush land. It was the most beautiful sight I had ever seen.

We stayed at the Park in these beautiful huts with netting to protect us from the mosquitoes. Ash had her own hut. In each hut was a bullhorn, in case we needed to alert the workers of an intrusion by an animal. It is so ironic that animals never scared me, only people. A giraffe observed us at our individual tables for breakfast. There was a native woman kneading dough for that night's dinner. All food was picked freshly the same day. It was not only amazing but also very peaceful. I cherished every moment. It was like being displaced from your home into the television and transported to the National Geographic network.

We had two safari rides a day and were promised to see all the five great animals and more. A sitting lion was five feet away with a tracker holding his rifle in place. I still felt the safest I had ever felt.

We were riding in our jeep and were told to cover our eyes; we were approaching a "spitting spider." They will blind you with their venom, we were told. Still no fear from me, but Jay almost hit the deck. It was really funny.

I absolutely found my place on earth in this peaceful paradise. Tranquility reigned there. I saw the most exquisite birds I'd ever laid eyes on. All in all, the place was a far cry from city life, filled with concrete and populated by pigeons that scrounged around your feet for scraps.

At night the skies had colors that only a painter's palate could envision. The purples, reds and yellows of the sky were magnificent. I could have stared at the sky all night.

We later visited Victoria Falls and ran through the mists of water that drenched us with joy.

Soon, it was time leave this paradise; we had to leave our daughter in the hands of Cape Town. Separation to me was still as scary as always. It still removed all feelings of safety and left me feeling like I was five years old again, waiting for my mother who forgot to pick me up. Yet we had to go and so we did.

Arriving Home

Ashley finished her time at Wisconsin and finally came home. She finally said the words I had been looking for: *"I think I had enough of being away."* Upon her arrival home, she asked me to make an appointment at the hair salon. It was in Manhattan. When the hairdresser removed the clip from her head, I literally almost fainted! There were patches of her scalp where there was no hair. I did not know what to do or say. We returned to the rheumatologist who we had seen before she left. Her thyroid level was very low and she was anemic. I asked privately if her hair would grow back. He said it would. To this day I will never understand her thought process of why she did not tell me about her hair loss.

Ashley then applied to a one year accelerated MSW program at Loyola University in Chicago. Ashley told me not to get my hopes up; over one hundred students had applied. Thirty students would be accepted. She was accepted!

Chicago was another new experience for me; life with Ashley was never boring. She was assigned to a dorm with two other girls who got there before we did. When you are not quick, you get the smallest room in the dorm. Ashley and I stand at five feet nine inches. Her legs literally touched the wall from one side to the other.

This was going to be another eye opening experience for my Ashy. Now instead of an all-white school she was attending a school with a much more diverse population. A much larger percentage of students than she had been accustomed to were African-American. Ashley had two roommates; one was a white Baptist from the South and the other was an African-American, also a Baptist from the South. One was a pig and the other was a hermit. That first weekend, Ash asked them to go on a communal food-shopping trip. Her roommates got different foods, none of which Ashley would eat. Ashley called me Sunday morning and was so upset. When she woke up, both her roommates were not there. She could not imagine why they would go out without her. Surprise! The two roommates were at church. They would continue to have bible readings in their dorm room. This is what occurs

194

when you interact with different cultures and religions. Ashley is Jewish, through and through.

Ashley had classes two days a week and needed to do three days of internship. She interned in a homeless shelter in downtown Chicago. Can these people not recognize a JAP (Jewish American Princess) when they see her? Pretty funny. This was way too disgusting for my daughter. I explained that this is what is required; it will only be for one term. In the middle of the term, Ash called me up to tell me she had bug bites all over her body. We thought she was having a flare-up. She closed her window and searched all over and saw nothing until the next morning; there were small dots of blood on her sheets.

Ashley brought home bed bugs from the shelter and they quickly spread to the other rooms. When she made the dorm head aware, he did nothing! Weeks went by and the crying continued. Life never went as smoothly as one imagined or hoped.

Ashley was yelling, *"What am I supposed to do? No one listens."* I told her to take pictures of her body and send them to me via text. Our next door neighbor in Bayside, Queens was an attorney. He told me to call the

Department of Health. That's what I did! The supervisor of the dorm house was not a happy camper. They actually blamed Ashley for bringing in the bed bugs. What did they expect she would bring home from a homeless shelter?

The dorm's personnel were instructed to have the whole apartment building checked for bed bugs. Ashley and her roommates had to wrap up all their clothing, bedding and towels to be sent to specific dry cleaners for handling bedbugs. A few new sets of clothing needed to be bought, while all her stuff was being cleaned. Seven thousand dollars later, Loyola had to accept responsibility for all expenses. New sets of guidelines were set on where the students would do their internships.

Ashley graduated with honors. Her plenty of scars are a reminder that, no matter who you are, no one gets out scar free.

Last Stop, All Off!

Never be fooled by a wolf in sheep's clothing.

That is exactly what happened to me in 2007. I was at my computer at school and read an ad from a new Principal opening a new alternative high school. The school would take in students aging out of high school who were not anywhere close to graduating. The Principal was sending out letters of recruitment for students that filled that description. I wrote her about a few of my students that were headed nowhere. She asked if she could meet me at my school and interview them. And so she did.

I was immediately entranced by her plans for her school. She wrote the grant and proposed it to the people that authorize such grants. There is so much money out there for schools and programs which wealthy people want to invest in for their tax write off. Besides, it looks really altruistic when you tell people that you are supporting a cause for education. It is extremely seductive to all involved, including myself.

197

I had been waiting my whole career to make a difference, without the typical bureaucracy knocking down ideas that will fund underprivileged students and make the playing field more level. What a ride! This Principal hired me on the spot. She promised me everything from private parking to a huge office with windows all around the suite. I would be given a brand new computer and all the money I wanted to decorate my new creative and enticing office. I immediately started working there the following fall.

I was able to get bagels and cream cheese from a local bagel merchant every day who gave me all the bagels that were not eaten the previous day so that I could feed my newly found students. I got a refrigerator to keep the milk and juices cold.

I couldn't believe what was happening; but I should not have been so naive to think it was really happening. With more strings attached than a Macy's Day parade balloon, it was only a matter of time before the Nor'easter came through to blow it all away.

The storm did not arrive for a while. The first year was blissful. Every wish was granted. The Principal was as sharp as a newly serrated blade. She was brave and belligerent. I became her right hand; anything she asked I did. She made me feel as though as I was the best counselor, and that she had won me in a poker game. She constantly praised me and filled the emotional holes that I had been craving for all my professional life. I hadn't known how astute she was, always picking up on people's weaknesses. Not just mine but everyone's.

There were only nine faculty hired that first year. The school was intimate and creative. We could use any techniques that would bring the students to school. And they were coming; her techniques were totally creative... and illegal. You see, the new school would be evaluated based on the students' attendance.

But what did I know about her rules? I was never an administrator. She never gave a thought about her "creativity." If a student attended regularly for one week without cutting school, they received a pair of Apple headphones worth three hundred dollars!!!

Word starting getting out that the students were getting extravagant gifts just for attending.

However, the powers that be were so impressed with our success rate that the Principal was asked to do interviews to explain how she had become so successful. Her sociopathic brain was taking in all those accolades. The more attention she received, the more she pushed the limits.

By the end of the school year, we were purchasing hundreds of dollars of food a month, most of which she took home. When refrigerators were ordered for the school, one went home to her house. I only learned of this from the people who began to talk. Everyone was in her pocket. Staff was receiving money for overtime without having to put in the hours; the custodial staff was getting loads of cash to redo her home on school time. Men were sexually harassed in the building. I was told to pick up her sixteen-year-old son from home to escort him to school.

The second year of school began, and I was making my annual visit to my oncologist. It was that day that he explained to me that the medicines I had been taking to reduce the chance of getting breast cancer would no longer be effective. Tamoxifen is only effective for five years, after which people have to look at other options. I could get a prophylactic double mastectomy or wait until I get breast cancer and then deal with the chemotherapy. My chances of getting breast cancer were increasing exponentially. Having the BRCA gene means that you would likely get cancer by the age of seventy. I was now fifty-two and had escaped my fate up until now.

After that meeting with the doctor, I had to make the decision whether or not to have the surgery before the cancer reared its ugly head. I had already seen the havoc that chemo wreaked on one's body and brain so I definitely wanted to avoid that. I finally decided on the double mastectomy.

I had confided in my principal who was very supportive. She reassured me that although I needed six weeks recuperation time, she would make sure the days did not come out of my attendance bank. I was thrilled and gladly accepted such a generous offer. The Principal's mother had died of cancer when she was young and she always cried when she spoke of her. She told me she would not be able to visit me but that she would call every day to see how I was.

This woman again seemed very incredible to me. She also had my favorite students call from her office to say hello and sent me hugs and kisses. She also sent flowers to the hospital. Never had I experienced such concern and compassion. The day I came back to school, she had the art department create a huge sign for me outside the school building welcoming me back home. Days were not subtracted from my bank and everything appeared to be wonderful.

Her son was a basketball player, and one day he made the local newspaper and I wanted to convey how proud I was of him. I hung up his article next to his picture outside of my office. When someone told her what I had done, she lost her freaking mind. She stormed down to my end of the hallway and ripped it off the wall. She began screaming at me in front of all the students and asserted that I was not his mother. According to her, only she had the right to hang up pictures of her son. I was upset and humiliated in front of the students. I could not sleep at all that evening. I discussed the situation with my husband and I decided to end our familiar relationship and keep it only on a professional basis. I would no longer allow her to berate me in front of staff or students. No matter what the cost.

I had no idea that a sociopath could turn so fast. Even my father would give me a warning before he flipped out on me. All my privileges were revoked. My parking spot was rescinded; I lost my dignity that I had worked so hard to gain, and most devastatingly, she turned my beloved students against me. Within one week, no one came to see me in my office anymore. She threatened them if they did. I could not believe this was happening to me.

Months passed and my feelings of self-worth plummeted. I tried everything I could to lure my students back. Nothing worked! I became depressed and felt so worthless. I confided in the person closest to her who I was friendly with what I had been feeling; his response was shocking and totally unexpected. *"What did you think? You were getting all these perks for free? Nothing is ever free!"*

I could not deal with the isolation at school; she lied to the faculty telling them that I confided in her about their lives. She made it appear that I was betraying their secrets. I was not able to tell anyone the truth. I never had the necessary courage. I never turned in my father, his psychiatrist, and the fraud perpetrated at the Veterans Hospital. I could have blown her up with all the knowledge I had, but I still held dearly to the code from the street to never snitch on anyone.

I was not proud of the wrongdoings of that last year and a half. I was not proud of being my father's comfort and accepting and liking it. Once again, I was in a shameful place and it was awful.

Taking a Losing Stand

I told my husband that I could no longer work for the Board of Education. I would do anything to make up for the financial loss of early retirement. We met with the UFT retirement expert to put in my papers. I must be one of the very few educators that cried at her decision to retire. Most educators jump for joy when they retire, but I was being hit with a thirty thousand dollar a year decrease due to leaving two years earlier than the twenty-five years in service requirement. This left me feeling like a victim once again.

I needed to reframe this for myself. I was so tired of being victimized. I needed to remind myself that I was resourceful and full of great ideas. All I had to do was choose one idea and make it work. I discussed this with two of my tennis teammates and they encouraged me to do what I know best.

I enrolled at Harlem Hospital and registered for classes in the Lactation Licensing program. I then signed up for classes to become a doula. A doula is a birth companion or post–birth supporter. I felt this was a natural transition for me as a caretaker. After two hundred hours of classes and experience in the field working with pregnant women, I was a Certified Doula. I love learning and growing. I started educating expectant mothers by playing breast-feeding jeopardy at the local Babies R Us. I volunteered to do this in hopes that I would get clients. I did this for a year. It was so much fun working with pregnant couples. However, it was not a strong enough pull to get private clients. It is expensive to hire a lactation counselor.

I still have my license and hope to continue in the future. I was not done however. Since that was not bringing in any income, I obviously needed to try something else.

Another strong love I have is for cooking food to feed others. Jay and I came up with the idea of making organic oatmeal. What an adventure it was! Jay and I started marketing my oatmeal with nine different flavors. We did some research together and I decided to start small to see if this was a viable option. So we bought an expandable table and I created a visually beautiful cart like table so that I could sell hot oatmeal at the Douglaston train station. I received grand reviews. People would yell, *"Wait for me, Oatmeal Lady!"* as they ran to the train. Jay and I worked all the time next to one another. Our business was growing and once again, I was experiencing Jay's support for my newest venture.

I felt so fulfilled in so many ways doing this. I loved Jay more and more. He would get up at five-thirty in the morning, pack up my wares and follow me to the train station before he left for work. Everyone seemed to think that my oatmeal was very delicious. I had five different toppings and three different flavors of oatmeal each morning, Monday to Friday. I would work each morning until eleven, until the last morning train left the station.

Coming home was somewhat daunting; I had to clean the pots and all the utensils. The fun part was counting the money each day.

Every morning I would see the same commuters who would buy my oatmeal and praise me for feeding them a wholesome meal to begin their day. After three months at the train station, one of my usual customers asked me if I would consider doing a food spot on Fox's morning show with Rosanna Scotto and Gregg Kelly. He happened to be one of the main cameramen. He told me that I would come off great on television, and maybe someone would pick my oatmeal to market. I was ecstatic.

Sweet revenge. Everyone was going to see me! I would be famous and successful. It was so exciting to go through the back stage door and have assistants help me set up the props and start cooking a large pot of apple pie oatmeal. It went off great and there I was on television. I believe I was as good as I could be, nervous as any novice. I think I came off friendly, warm and appealing. At the end of the cooking spot, all the camera people and all the extras started an enormous line to get a bowl of my oatmeal. This was an unreal experience.

It started to work. Stores offered to pay me for my oatmeal, but wanted to use the store's name. I declined that offer; if I was going to kill myself in preparation of my oatmeal, then it is my name that should appear on the product, Simply Randi's Oatmeal. Many local newspaper articles were written about me.

We then decided to take the show on the road. We went to Riverhead Organic Indoor Market every Saturday and Sunday to sell quarts of our organic oatmeal at $15 a pop, but found it was too tiresome to do both days at fifty miles each way. Working one day with great profit was so satisfying. We had our regulars and new people were a blast. As a couple we had fun running a business together. We had a plan, and it fed our basic needs of making money for our kids. We wanted to make enough money to give our kids a down payment for their first home. We were making around fifteen thousand a year. We were successful as long as we stayed in Queens, which ultimately changed.

Two Became Four!

Monday evenings I played in a women's doubles tennis league. This particular Monday, my daughter called up and asked if she and her new husband of eleven months could come over for dinner. Ash stated that she was too tired after her day at New York Presbyterian Hospital as a Social Worker in the Urology Department to make dinner. I was suspicious and told Jay that Ash is pregnant, or else she would never ask me to miss tennis. We both started to cry, even before they got to us. Ash and Daniel walked in and she handed me a Tupperware container that she said she was returning. When I opened it, it contained her positive pregnancy test. We could not have been more thrilled.

I have not mentioned my son-in-law before. He is a mother's dream for a son-in-law. Educated in the same field of Social Work, he once bought an elderly woman a shawl because she was cold. Dan worked in the burn unit at the same hospital as Ash. Dan also befriended a young

Ecuadorian young man who had been burnt over ninety percent of his body. He was fixing his carburetor when it sparked and blew up. Dan found a burn victim seminar that was held for doctors in this field that he thought would be a valuable experience for his patient. It was quite far away, but Dan drove him there and back. His patient was so appreciative. Daniel is a very unique young man, thoughtful and sensitive to others' needs. There was a patient who would only eat vegan; Dan went to a vegan restaurant for one of this man's last meals.

Dan has two older sisters. That meant to me that he had already been trained to deal with all sorts of female hysteria! Daniel is creative and loves working with his hands building and creating furniture. A Jew who builds is an enigma in itself. He was handsome enough for my beautiful daughter and oh was I thrilled at the thought of the beautiful children they would have.

Two weeks later they walked into my house crying. I had to hold on to the wall. I naturally thought Ash had had a miscarriage. I could barely believe it when Dan showed me a book titled "What to Do When You Are Having Two." I threw the book down and said, *"Get the fuck outta here!"* Their crying had not slowed down. Ash said, *"I only wanted one baby. How could this happen?"* No twins run in our family or Dan's. They were just beginning their careers and money was tight. Oh my goodness, I was thinking. So we will have to help.

That was the beginning of one nightmarish pregnancy. Genetic testing showed an abnormality in one of the twin's facial structure, and Ash tested positive for carrying the mutation for Cystic Fibrosis. If Dan was a carrier, one of the babies would definitely have this dreaded disease. He ran that same day to get tested. Every test took an insurmountable amount of time to come back with answers. Dan came out negative for the disease. It was crying bouts one after another with many what-ifs that almost drove us mad with worries. I was being tortured as a mother to come up with words of reassurance and wise words. I cried each day, praying "please don't do this to my daughter." It did not help one bit. It was terrible and frightening. I did not think things could be worse! They were supposed to be happy with anticipation, not scared out of their minds of what kind of babies would be born.

In the twenty-seventh week of pregnancy, Ash called me on the phone and told me she was having contractions. I reassured her that this was Braxton Hicks (pre-term contractions), nothing to be concerned about. I told her to call the doctor, and the doctor also told her the same thing. After hours of increasing contractions, they went to Lenox Hill Hospital and were admitted. The doctors said she was definitely in labor, and they would try to stop the labor with a cocktail of interventions. The contractions slowed down but did not stop.

A day later, Dan called us in the middle of the night and told us to hurry up to the hospital. My poor baby! We drove so fast; it felt like we were there in ten minutes (it was actually forty). It was too late. They already did the C-section and Ash was in recovery. I felt like this was an out of body experience. How and why was I going to explain all that had happened to my already exhausted and traumatized baby?

The twins were born at two pounds each exactly, a boy and a girl. Ashley could not see her twins for two days, leaving her feeling so detached from the babies. So unprepared for a whole new level of life and new motherhood. I never left her side or the babies. Neither did Dan or Jay. The doctors explained that all this was going to be very challenging and scary. Abraham seemed so much more delicate then Zadie. Blood transfusions and infections were not helping him grow. Ashley and Daniel never left those babies in fear that they would not be present for one of the tests that would be performed. They looked like zombies and were more exhausted then I think two people could be. But they had each other. They took turns comforting each other by saying *"This is going to be all right."* They took turns crying and praying. Daniel is brave and optimistic, but even this was too difficult at times. Skin to skin was given all day and half way into the night. They could not be taken away from their babies.

For three inconceivable months, day in and day out, Ash and Dan held those babies, literally for their life. Ashley pumped her milk every two hours. She was more exhausted then anyone I have ever seen. They worked like a machine to do what they felt needed to be done. My daughter and son-in-law are survivors and troopers beyond all imagination.

These babies had already lived a life that probably should have never happened. They are the products of pure dedication and persistency. I knew these babies had to thrive with the amount of love they were given every minute of their tiny lives, since the moment they were pulled from my daughter's belly.

With Every Traumatic Event a New Direction is Created!

Dan and Ash had taken a leave from work at the hospital to be with their babies. Food and shelter did not matter! Dan is the brave one in this newly created family. Ash's father, Jay, thinks risks are scary and if you are lucky enough to secure a union job, you keep it, he had taught Ashley. Dan believes in taking chances, especially when you are as talented as the two of them are. Dan's plan was to create a private practice with just the two of them. It would meet the needs of his family just fine. This way the babies would never be without a parent on any given day. Dan was clinically trained to work with challenging kids. His insights are accurate and so well executed. Ashley was trained in Family and Marriage Counseling at the Adlerian Institute postgraduate school. They both had their own set of gifts for their family, work and the world we live in.

And So it Goes

When the babies were finally allowed to come home, they were faced with a new set of concerns. Abe couldn't keep his food down at all. He didn't gain weight and Ash continued to lose weight. This became a serious issue. Of course I could understand what she was feeling and experiencing, but these circumstances did not put her in the best fighting shape. This fight was not for a featherweight and Ash needed to eat to continue. That didn't happen and Abe did not eat either. Ash and Dan never got more than a couple of hours of sleep per day. How long could they sustain this before they broke down? Jay and I sold our home in Queens and decided to rent an apartment within walking distance from the kids. They needed us and we needed them. We did all we could. It was never enough. This job was meant for more than four adults. Abe was so difficult to soothe and comfort. We never knew what to do for him. Anxiety continued and we were treading on glass with one another.

217

Cleaning, cooking, pep talks, showers, pumping and doctor appointments, hospital visits and state evaluators. Remaining optimistic was harder than I thought it could be. It was not ending. How were we going to get through this?

The Power of Love

A year and a half later, things started to get better and we gained some perspective on what had become our new norm. The babies were growing slowly, but they were growing! The tears were coming less frequently. The question still remained, *"Are the babies going to be okay?"* Their personalities became apparent and when the metamorphosis happened, they became so physically beautiful. It was like watching Benjamin Button turn human. When our grandbabies were born looking like old Martians it was so hard to imagine how they would look down the line. Needless to say, they became breathtaking to us.

Ash and Dan's practice was becoming successful and they purchased their first home.

Jay and Me

I have never had the privilege to watch anyone's marriage evolve positively, not my parents, grandparents or anyone that was in my familiar circle. Watching a long-term marriage grow successfully can be a beautiful but frustrating journey, but at least you have an idea what is coming and how to deal with problems when they arise. No one ever talks about the reality of what happens to a partnership over the years. You get accustomed to it one way and then aging starts to slowly creep into your life and you say to yourself, *"What now?"*

It would be so valuable to have learned what it feels like when your spouse gets older and can no longer be on the neighborhood basketball team. That takes a shot at your vitality as a man. What occurs when one or both retires? Everyone must learn the new dance so that the steps of life's events don't throw you out of kilter.

Jay is the kind of man that loves to be productive. He would not be capable of finding a hobby, because in his core beliefs, playing is not working and working makes you productive, even to the end. Jay was at the right place at the right time. Just after he retired, he was asked to fill a position at Lehman College as an administrator. He was so fortunate that he remains there presently fifteen years later. He has maintained his self-worth and value. He continues to see the impact he makes on students all the time.

On the other hand, with myself, I continue to sustain myself at just above water level. I am not quite fulfilled, except in my role as mother, grandmother, wife and daughter. I am very competent at those roles, I have been trained since five years of age. I would like to see myself as an avid tennis player, decorator and head cook! At least, the dream is still alive.

Being displaced from Queens to the Bronx has made my goals even harder to reach. My life for the past two and a half years has been on hold until we make our final move to Danbury, Connecticut. I imagine that is where I will make new friends and set up a new place to live out the joy I foresee. It should feel great to be in a place of self-assurance and beauty, which I never experienced in my younger years. It really is a strange feeling to feel things that you should have felt years ago, however 1 have finally arrived at a place of acceptance and real gratitude. My back hurts when I cook too long, I can play doubles tennis for two hours straight and feel younger and more desirable than ever. But those knees remind me: hey, you sixty-one year old, take it easy. Sometimes I am sure that the trauma or all those years of self-hatred and no real placement has dissipated and has been replaced by positivity.

I have so much to be thankful for; my twenty-five year marriage that has been life changing tops my gratitude list. Jay has forever changed me by loving me in a way that feels good, not hurtful. He has never lied to me that I know of. My daughter is a better woman and mother because of the fine example of this union that we have set. Jay has been more than my stabilizer; his voice is one of reason and calmness, even when the tides are coming fast and furious. He always remains in control.

Life, as I have lived it, has not been an easy one. There have been ups and down and the going often got rough. However, I survived everything with the help of Jay and my daughter. It was not a life of dreams for Jay or for me, but I guess in the world two bodies collided and found love and peace – this made for a reality which is better than any dream I could have dreamed for myself.

Final Journey

January 19, 2018. Danbury CT. One month after leaving Riverdale, Bronx, mom was complaining that her shoulder hurt her. I explained away her anxiety with a theory that it hurt her because she was doing her chair exercises with too much vigor. After one week, I relented and found a doctor at the most respected hospital in town, Danbury Hospital. They sent us to another doctor.

A thirty-five-year-old very attractive doctor walked in and his eyes only engaged with mom's. After years of traveling with mom to all sorts of physicians who only spoke directly to me, and discarded my mom as someone who could not care for herself, this doctor was very different. That one trait placed him high on my list for not minimalizing my very independent and competent mom. After an extremely thorough exam, he explained that her shoulder was not hurting her due to excessive exercise.

I began to feel sweaty and anxious. My mind was going to scary places, which I did not want to visit. The doctor proceeded to fill out a prescription pad for her to receive a body scan. I am always on top of things. So, the appointment was set for the following day.

A technician came out to the waiting area with the medical reports that were faxed over by the previous doctor. The technician and the rest of the medical team decided and informed us that her heart was too weak for the contrast dye. They decided just to do a body scan without contrast.

Within twenty-four hours, my life would never be the same. Not in the way I visualized the next few months. We were to be moving into a brand new home with a whole new apartment for mom. Neither one of us had ever lived in something that others had not decimated or had left their human footprints on. This is what we had been waiting for. We had left Riverdale after two and half years of living in what was perceived as a "beautiful neighborhood" but was anything but that. You see for the first year and half I only saw my world through tears as Jay and I walked to and fro to our daughter's apartment to help care for our grandchildren and daughter and son-in-law. Nothing else mattered or existed. We were all in zombie like states performing anything and everything humanly possible to make those babies thrive and survive.

In January of 2017 Ash and Dan found their new home and lead their healthy family to begin a new life 75 minutes away from us. However, with their new start it left me with no purpose, no friends and nothing but time waiting for our new home to be built.

Mommy was diagnosed with stage four breast cancer, with its destructive cells circulating to each organ and eventually her bones, stealing our dream, my dream to provide the ultimate oasis for her final years.

Mommy and I had spent hours and days looking at new furnishings, web sites and dreaming of making new connections. Our new life in Connecticut would consist of me making her life carefree of all the things that haunted her. No more intimidation, no more poverty and most importantly no more feeling less deprived than anyone else. Mom was 85 years young when she expired on March 3, 2018. Never will she experience what I promised her!

Epilogue

One of my major neuroses in my life is always reviewing and checking in on my mind's eye. Am I living correctly? Could I have been more pro-active on working on myself? More diligent in the way I mothered? How I carried myself at work? Been a better sister? I am not easy to penetrate, nor easy to become friends with. It is not easy for me to forgive or embrace if you have deceived me. I have lived my life like I wanted others to treat me. I must accept the fact that in my early years I was not equipped with the skills I needed to prevent me from being a victim. Everyone around me was a victim. Victims of ignorance, poverty, poor values, lack of education, little respect for people or property.

I have dedicated my life to trying to protect others. Successful or not, the intent was there. One can analyze if I was trying to give back to myself. I must be honest in that of course I would have wanted the things for myself that I gave or provided to others. That does not detract from the value of giving and wanting others to experience what others had not given to me.

My legacy has always been one of growth, no matter what kind. It is more difficult than others will admit to you. Challenging beyond belief. But it can be done.

Made in the USA
Middletown, DE
01 May 2018